Frid Framework™ for Enterprise Knowledge Management

Frid Framework™ for Enterprise Knowledge Management

A Common KM Framework for the Government of Canada

Knowledge-Enabled Business Management

Dr. Randy J Frid

iUniverse, Inc.
New York Lincoln Shanghai

Frid Framework™ for Enterprise Knowledge Management
A Common KM Framework for the Government of Canada

iUniverse, Inc.

For information address:
iUniverse, Inc.
2021 Pine Lake Road, Suite 100
Lincoln, NE 68512
www.iuniverse.com

ISBN: 0-595-30699-3

Printed in the United States of America

Dedicated to the memory of my grandmother, Winnifred Robertson, for her love of life, her passion and commitment to nature, and for making the world a better place to live for people and animals alike. I think it only fitting that I'm also dedicating this book to my best friend Bobby whom I'm sure my grandmother is taking care of right now.

CONTENTS

TABLE OF ILLUSTRATIONS

PREFACE

The Canadian Institute of Knowledge Management (CIKM) believes that knowledge management (KM) is really *knowledge-enabled business management*. This practical and straightforward approach to KM is embodied within CIKM's Frid Framework™ for Enterprise Knowledge Management. This document outlines the framework and provides a common-sense, business-focused approach to KM.

The framework is flexible and enables organizations to implement only those components they need. Each of the framework's constituent components delivers value; it is not necessary to implement the entire framework for organizations to appreciate the significant return on investment KM delivers.

The framework's architecture provides for both a top-down and bottom-up approach to implementation.

In a best-case scenario, the framework is implemented according to the top-down approach laid out in this document. However, should this approach not be feasible, implementation of the KM Analysis Process (bottom-up approach) alone will generate value and start to implant knowledge engineering into organizational culture. The remainder of the framework can be implemented incrementally.

The framework is not intended to provide answers to all knowledge-management questions; rather, it is a practical beginning—a starting point that embodies the principles, rules, conventions, standards, values and procedures that will enable organizations to measure and manage their growing investments in the intangible corporate resources commonly referred to as *Intellectual Assets*.

The Frid Framework™ is still evolving, and will likely continue to do so for many years. This book is intended to inspire additional critical thinking and debate.

Dr. Randy Frid

1. KM: THE BUSINESS ENABLER

Knowledge management incorporates management of intellectual assets and is the next generation of business management. The Canadian Institute of Knowledge Management (CIKM) refers to KM as *knowledge-enabled business management*.

1.1. What are Intellectual Assets?

Intellectual assets include:

- People — knowledge, experience, expertise, capability, creativity, capacity, relationships and networks; and

- Process — formalized business processes; and

- Intellectual Property — Patents, Trademarks, Branding, etc… Basically, anything defensible by law.

These assets have common properties in that they are intangible, have perceived value that can only be recognized when transacted, and are not measured by Generally Accepted Accounting Principles (GAAP) other than recognizing basic costs or winding up in the Good Will slush fund.

1.2. What is KM and why should I care?

1.2.1. Knowledge management is a key enabler of modern comptrollership

The Government of Canada (GoC) is actively engaged in modern comptrollership, an initiative to modernize management practices across the federal public service. By focusing on sound resource management, rigorous stewardship, informed decision-making, improved risk management, appropriate control systems, and shared ethical practices and values, modern comptrollership ensures that federal departments are fiscally responsible, results-oriented and responsive to the needs of Canadians. Effective modern comptrollership should lead to better programs and services, enhanced public policy, and improved results for Canadians.

The GoC's modern comptrollership approach involves building a solid foundation of modern management practices within government departments and agencies, and enable informed decision-making by providing easily accessible, comprehensive and accurate information to decision makers.

Modern comptrollership is not about increased control; rather, it is about providing managers with the tools and training that enable them to prioritize, plan and meet operational goals. The GoC initiative goes beyond financial control and accounting, involving all departmental employees and necessitating fundamental changes to the corporate culture of the public service.

Departments throughout the GoC are beginning to understand the fundamental necessity of adopting business-management strategies that incorporate effective management of intellectual assets—some of the GoC's primary and most prevalent resources.

1.2.2. Knowledge Management is not Information Management

At a time when stewardship of government knowledge is as important to Canadian citizens as management of any other public resource, it's apparent that many GoC organizations are still focused on Information Management (IM).

The difference between IM and KM is simple: IM delivers information; KM helps manage what people do with information.

Even in a total absence of information, decisions are made. However, such decisions are not likely to be informed. Information—and, more importantly, knowing what to do with it—is key to informed decision-making.

1.2.3. Knowledge management is not technology—it's management

When information technology was introduced into the business world a few decades ago, organizations already had solid understanding of management principles, measurements and metrics. Information technology was employed to help implement and perform these tasks more efficiently.

However, KM technologies are being adopted before organizations have developed a mature management infrastructure—one that deals with management of intellectual assets. KM technologies are being employed before organizations fully understand what efficiencies they are tying to achieve, how to align KM initiatives across an enterprise, and how to justify KM expenditures.

KM initiatives have been successful in many organizations around the world, but few have proven sustainable. Typically, successes have been driven by CEO-mandated change. KM initiatives typically fade and die without direct leadership. Sustainable KM initiatives require infrastructure and integration. Without a solid management framework that is integrated into day-to-day business-management practices, KM will produce only sporadic benefits and questionable results.

Within a solid management framework, IT is harnessed to provide access to information, and to help scale KM efforts to:

- enhance decision making;
- build bridges between islands of knowledge;
- manage knowledge trade relations;
- identify new islands of knowledge;
- leverage knowledge already created;
- prepare the next generation of information worker; and
- stimulate innovative thinking.

1.2.4. What will KM do for you?

Knowledge management provides organizations with a methodical approach to managing their knowledge requirements and assets.

By adopting KM as a set of sound management principles, rules, conventions, standards, values and procedures, organizations can measure and manage their growing investments in intellectual assets. These are assets over which organizations have historically had little control—until now.

Every day, decisions are made in response to organizational questions:

- How should troop movements be altered in response to this threat?

- Should these documents be shredded?

- What government program should be recommended to the child of an Alzheimer's patient?

- How should this new policy be introduced?

Sometimes individuals make decisions in response to their own questions; sometimes they respond to questions from other people such as external clients, citizens and suppliers. Whatever the source of the question, people are making decisions that define their organizations.

Government of Canada departments typically manage explicit information (data) well, with robust processes and sophisticated frameworks. However, decisions are made even when in the absence of appropriate questions, adequate knowledge, and understanding of the importance of related information. Many of these decisions will influence an organization's products, services, clients, partners, allies and enemies alike.

Without a structured work environment, there is no way to know what decisions are being made and when. There is no way to know whether the right questions are being asked. There is no way to know which type of information decision makers need, or how and when to make it available to them.

In a structured environment, however, corporate objectives are clearly defined and managers have a good understanding of how their processes work. Therefore, educated assumptions can be made about what people need to know, and when. Corporate 'survival of the fittest' also predicates an ongoing need to stimulate new thinking within organizational core competencies. As business requirements have reasonably well-defined boundaries, it is possible to extrapolate that there should be a clear and methodical approach to managing knowledge requirements and assets.

1.2.5. What do organizations need to manage?

On an enterprise scale, KM maturity needs to be managed and measured. KM maturity is the level of progress an organization is making toward implementing solid knowledge-management practices on a business-unit by business-unit basis. Integrating KM practices is the same as integrating other good business-management or project-management practices.

Within any specific business unit, knowledge management works on discrete business processes (problem/solution sets).

Within a discrete business process, an organization tries at a minimum to manage and measure:

- whether people are asking the right questions;

- what people know;

- what people don't know;

- how to best leverage people's knowledge;

- how to convince people to share knowledge;

- how to map what people know to a business process;

- how to fill knowledge gaps;

- how to capture and codify unique knowledge;

- how to prevent knowledge loss unless such a loss is 'planned abandonment';

- to whom or what to turn when people need to fill a knowledge gap;

- how to get people the knowledge they need, when they need it;

- how to repair knowledge processes if they fail;

- how to institutionalize successful knowledge processes;

- how to capture and advocate lessons learned and best practices; and

- how to value unique and proprietary corporate knowledge.

Efficient management within a solid KM framework facilitates effective stewardship of corporate knowledge assets. KM ensures that corporate knowledge can be retained, shared and re-used to benefit individuals and organizations alike. The ultimate goal of KM is to facilitate better decision-making and thereby to improve the quality of internal processes and service delivery to customers.

2. KM: The Danger Signs

Knowledge management is arguably one of the most valuable, cost-effective and efficient management tools in business today. Yet, today's knowledge-management practices are little used and, without a change of direction, will likely disappear as quickly as BPR, TQM and many similar management fads did in the past.

Given its obvious organizational value and huge return on investment, why is knowledge management, and in particular the way it's viewed and implemented today, on a path to extinction?

To address this question, it's necessary to trace the evolution of KM.

The forefather of today's knowledge management is Peter Drucker, who is also the father of modern management. A short time ago, with a simple yet powerful sweep of his pen, Drucker proclaimed that knowledge was the currency of the new world economy.

Naturally, business leaders around the world wanted to control this new currency. Powerful business leaders used their influence to drive reform based on leveraging knowledge assets and, in the early days, knowledge management experienced some high profile victories. These victories, however, were due not to sound management, but were driven by leadership alone, and by leaders who achieved organizational objectives at any cost. Many widely-published case studies on these initial knowledge-management victories indicate that they were generally the direct result of single-person, objective-driven leadership, rather than sound management.

The early successes proved to be false and dangerous—there is an enormous and fundamental difference between powerful leadership and sound management.

2.1. KM is not about leadership—it's about management

When people think of leadership, they generally think in terms of inspired individuals, individuals others willingly follow. When such a leader loses momentum, however, so do his or her followers. Leadership is a human quality; one that benefits from human ambition, but that also suffers from human weaknesses. Leadership conquers new frontiers while 'management' sustains and develops what has already been conquered.

To be successful, an organization needs both inspired leadership and sound management.

While leadership can best be described with dynamic verbs, management is best described by a set of universally accepted nouns: principles, rules, conventions, standards, values and procedures.

More importantly, management is sustainable, repeatable and measurable, while leadership is generally unique to an individual leader.

Generally Accepted Accounting Principles (GAAP) are used not to inspire or manage leadership but to manage assets; the same is true of knowledge management. Like GAAP, KM manages and measures assets—just a different type of asset than those GAAP was designed to manage.

Not long ago, intangible assets were of insignificant value compared to tangible assets. Today, knowledge is one of the world's most valuable commodities. Organizations are overwhelmed by technologies that enable real-time global transactions, by competition from all sides, by information overload, by 24x7 access to global intelligence, and by surging demand from citizens, suppliers, clients and employees to provide greater access to information and to allow more interaction in decision making. As a result, an unprecedented business demand has emerged for some form of structured rationalization process that can 'box in' organizational requirements, and justify time and money investments in knowledge-based technologies and initiatives.

If GAAP could manage intangible assets, knowledge management would not be needed.

2.2. Why aren't current KM practices working?

Current knowledge-management practices aren't working because today's knowledge management is not about management; rather, it's about knowledge theory and technological drivers—the complete opposite to what it should be.

Too many current knowledge-management practices are concerned with academic pursuit of the meaning of knowledge. Real-world executives, however, have little interest in the meaning of knowledge; rather, they view it is as another corporate asset that must be managed, measured and leveraged for maximum return on investment.

2.3. Making KM practices work successfully

As with any other corporate resource, such as cash, inventory, plant and equipment, organizations need to demonstrate to shareholders or citizens that they have the stewardship skills to manage knowledge. To accomplish this, some universally accepted principles, rules, conventions, standards, values and procedures need to be developed and adopted. Such a universally accepted framework will provide a solid foundation to manage and report intangible assets in the same way GAAP provides a foundation to manage tangible assets and liabilities while also reporting credible, concise, transparent and understandable financial information.

Knowledge-management practices must align with the demands of organizations, and the shareholders or citizens they serve. KM needs to communicate the messages executives want to hear. KM also needs to deliver the results that executives want to see. Organizations must adopt a sustainable, repeatable and measurable KM framework before they can expect to produce results in a consistent and comparable fashion.

2.4. KM must evolve—or die

Executives in both public and private sectors have little time for academic conversation or unsubstantiated requests for funding. Many managers also recall other self-proclaimed wonder-management strategies that promised much—and failed to deliver.

The term knowledge management will likely disappear from corporate lexicons unless KM practices realign to become relevant to today's real-world economics. However, even if the term knowledge management ceases to exist, intellectual assets will remain and the demand for effective and efficient ways to measure and manage these assets will continue to grow and evolve.

The CIKM's KM framework provides a way for KM practices to evolve and work successfully—and become effective and relevant management tools for today's executives.

3. KM: A GAME PLAN

3.1. Step 1—Adopt a framework

To develop a sustainable knowledge-management implementation, organizations need to adopt a solid KM framework.

A KM framework provides concepts, solution elements, implementation processes, and a structured method of managing organizations' intellectual assets and knowledge environment.

The Canadian Institute of Knowledge Management recommends use of the Frid Framework™ for Enterprise KM. The following illustration demonstrates the fundamental principles upon which the framework is built.

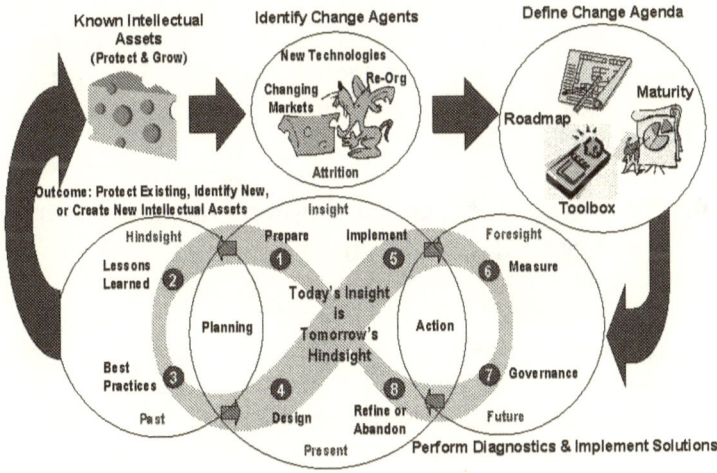

ILLUSTRATION 1: THE FRID FRAMEWORK™ FOR ENTERPRISE KM

The framework establishes a widely accepted set of rules, conventions, standards and procedures to manage and report on intellectual assets.

3.1.1. Known intellectual assets (protect and grow)

Intellectual assets are a recognized and integral part of the global economy. These assets must be managed with the same rigour as other capital assets such as cash, plant, equipment and inventories. Current intellectual assets must be protected; growth of new assets should be encouraged. Knowledge assets should be treated like cash assets and leveraged for maximum return on investment.

3.1.2. Identify change agents

Intellectual assets are susceptible to loss, depreciation and theft. The framework identifies and analyzes the change agents that specifically affect intellectual assets, thereby mitigating risk.

3.1.3. Define change agenda (infrastructure to support KM initiatives)

The framework establishes a change agenda that enables management to undertake discrete KM initiatives throughout organizations. The change agenda is comprised of a KM maturity model, roadmap and toolbox. CIKM recommends that the change agenda be implemented and managed from a central body known as the Knowledge Management Office (KMO), which provides governance and organizational alignment.

3.1.4. Perform diagnostics and implement solutions (repeatable and sustainable KM initiatives)

Once the change agenda is established, the framework provides a sustainable, repeatable diagnostic process that is implemented on an initiative-by-initiative basis. The outputs of the diagnostic process are two discrete deliverable documents (the KM Discovery Report and KM Recommendations Report). Each report provides independent value should no further action be taken. However, these reports can also be moved forward to the Solution Implementation process, which embodies knowledge-based components and terminology while following traditional project-management methodologies.

3.1.5. Outcomes

Discovery, creation and protection of intellectual assets are all potential outcomes of the framework.

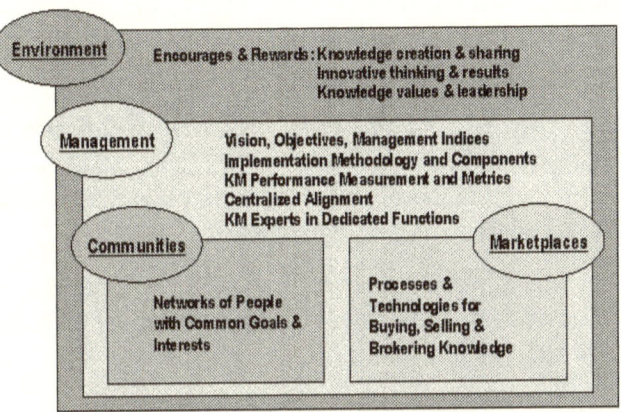

ILLUSTRATION 2: THE FRID FRAMEWORK™ COMPONENTS

The framework embodies management of the systematic and ongoing creation, sustainment, application, sharing, renewal and abandonment of knowledge that is integrated within business processes across an enterprise.

The framework augments traditional business management by employing a suite of knowledge-based tools that enable managers to assess their businesses and analyze business issues from a different perspective than the one provided by traditional tools such as GAAP. KM provides another layer in the ongoing evolution of business management.

Charles Darwin and Peter Drucker both proclaim—though from different perspectives—that it's neither the strongest of the species (or corporations) that will survive, nor the most intelligent, but rather those most responsive to change.

Innovation and improved decision-making—the key agents of change—are the prime targets of knowledge management, and are embodied within the framework.

3.2.   Step 2—Perform a maturity baseline

Before any organizational journey is undertaken, it's useful to know an enterprise's current position. This status check, or baseline, enables managers to decide where the organization needs to go and, more importantly, how to get there.

A KM maturity baseline measures the level of integration of knowledge-management processes within an organization's discrete business units. The KM baseline will take maturity readings on 36 interrelated management indices that measure progress in achieving the six goals of KM implementation.

The measurements can be repeated at regular intervals to assess progress against the initial baseline, providing management with crucial performance indicators.

3.3.   Step 3—Establish a knowledge-management office (KMO)

A KMO is crucial to establishing centralized KM alignment and integration across an enterprise.

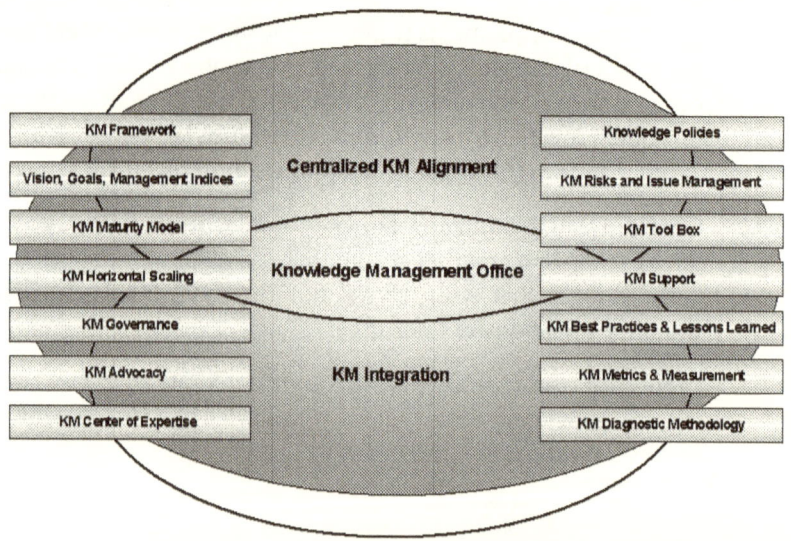

ILLUSTRATION 3: KNOWLEDGE MANAGEMENT OFFICE FUNCTIONS

3.4.   Step 4—Define a KM roadmap

With data from the KM maturity baseline, executives can decide organizational direction. To ensure the correct path is followed, an enterprise roadmap and, if necessary, additional roadmaps for subentities within the organization are established. The lowest level of granularity recommended for development of roadmaps is the discrete business unit.

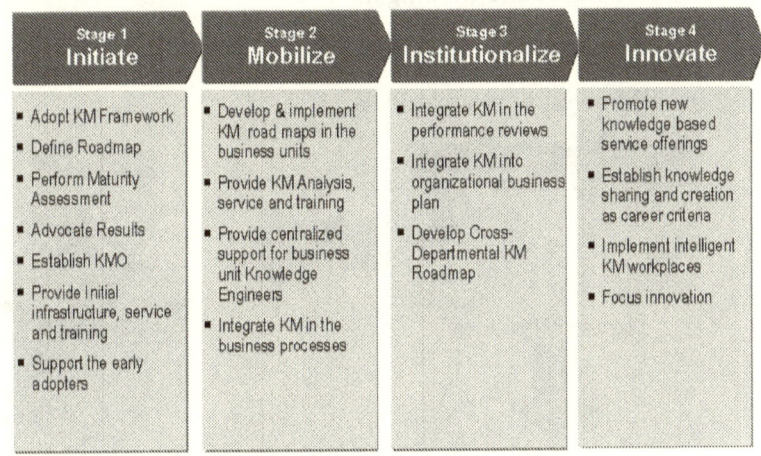

ILLUSTRATION 4: ENTERPRISE KM ROADMAP

3.5.   Step 5—Build a centralized KM toolbox

A centralized toolbox that an entire organization can access should be established and managed by the KMO. At a minimum, the toolbox should contain:

- a KM framework guide;
- KM policies;
- a KM maturity model;
- a KM analysis process;
- KM best practices;
- KM lessons learned;

- a KM discussion forum;

- a KM document repository;

- KM contacts;

- KM risk-, issue- and opportunity-management tools;

- KM links;

- KM guides and training materials;

- KM templates; and

- KM presentation materials.

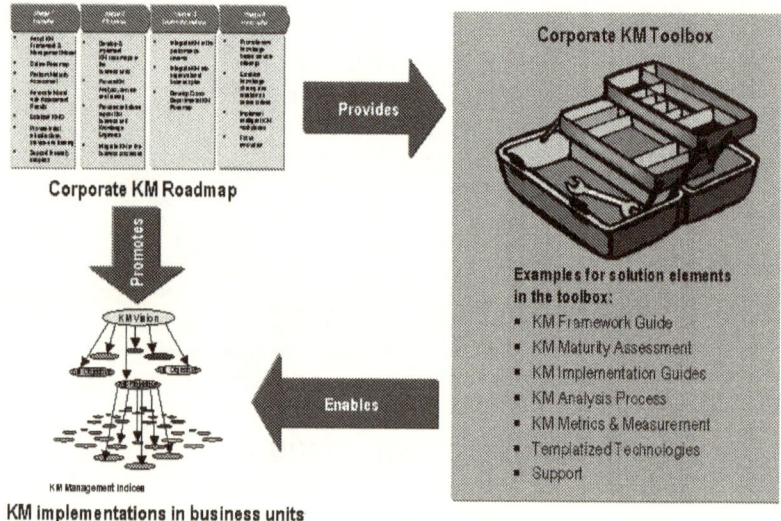

ILLUSTRATION 5: KM TOOLBOX INTEGRATION

3.6.   Step 5—Perform diagnostics and implement solutions

Once the KM infrastructure is prepared, organizations can begin to implement individual KM initiatives.

The KM analysis process enables managers to evaluate how organizational knowledge is mapped to business processes and relates to business drivers. The product of this process is a systematic rationalization of knowledge assets and requirements.

4. THE FRID FRAMEWORK™ MANAGEMENT MODEL

The Frid Framework™ management model encompasses:

1. KM vision: Where do we want to go?

2. KM objectives: How do we get there?

3. KM management indices: Where are we now?

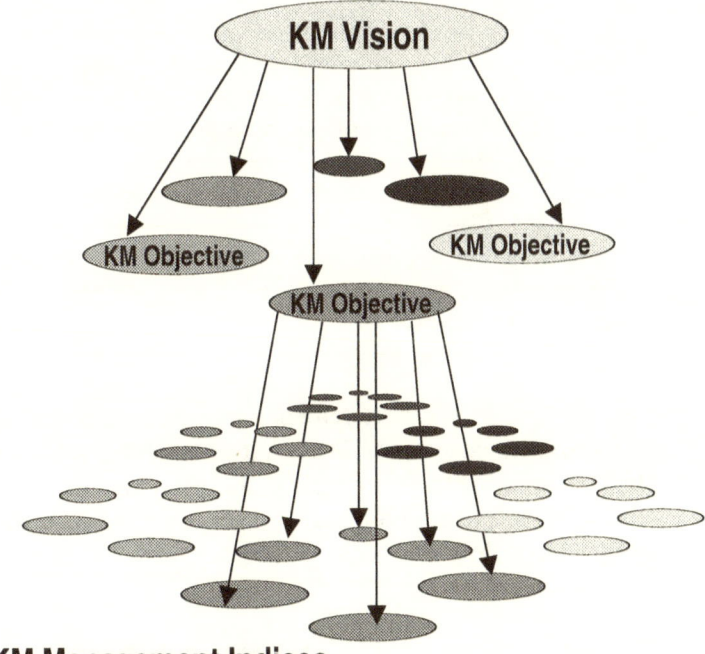

ILLUSTRATION 6: THE FRID FRAMEWORK™ MANAGEMENT MODEL

17

4.1. KM vision—Where do we want to go?

A vision should be simple to remember, understand and tell others about. However, a vision must also embody all of the values, qualities and attributes that will produce the desired outcome. A successful vision, effectively communicated, will enable employees at all organizational levels to describe it when asked. Developing a simple and effective vision, and undertaking the significant communication efforts required to propagate that vision go hand-in-hand. One without the other is useless; together they can move mountains and change the future.

CIKM's vision statement is: Helping people work together better.

On the surface, the statement seems simple, yet displays surprising elegance when each word is analyzed individually:

Helping	Teaching, mentoring, sharing, collaborating.
People	Managing and supporting human decision-making processes.
Work	Embedding KM into culture and processes.
Together	Team building.
Better	Positive change.

CIKM's simple vision statement embodies the heart and soul of knowledge management. KM is about teaching, mentoring, sharing and collaborating to help people make better and faster decisions. KM is also about team building and transferring knowledge among employees during the course of everyday work.

4.2. KM objectives—How do we get there?

Once a vision of what knowledge management can do for organizations has been developed, the question becomes: How do we get there?

The vision is achieved by incorporating into organizations six objectives for KM implementation:

Objective 1: Knowledge planning—embedding KM into organizational planning.

Objective 2: Knowledge retention—embedding KM into human resources.

Objective 3: Knowledge tools—KM technologies, implementation and collaboration.

Objective 4: Knowledge culture—building bridges between islands of knowledge.

Objective 5: Knowledge processes—embedding KM into process engineering.

Objective 6: Knowledge sharing and re-use—leveraging intellectual assets.

Each objective produces a clear outcome:

Objective 1: Knowledge planning. Outcome—alignment of knowledge to business drivers.

Objective 2: Knowledge retention. Outcome—prevents lost knowledge.

Objective 3: Knowledge tools. Outcome—provides scalability and sustainment.

Objective 4: Knowledge culture. Outcome—builds a sharing and learning environment.

Objective 5: Knowledge processes. Outcome—mitigates risk.

Objective 6: Knowledge sharing and re-use. Outcome—enhances return on investment of intellectual assets.

Embodied within each objective are four control functions:

1. Maturity—progress level of implementation.

2. Performance measurement.

3. Governance.

4. Valuation.

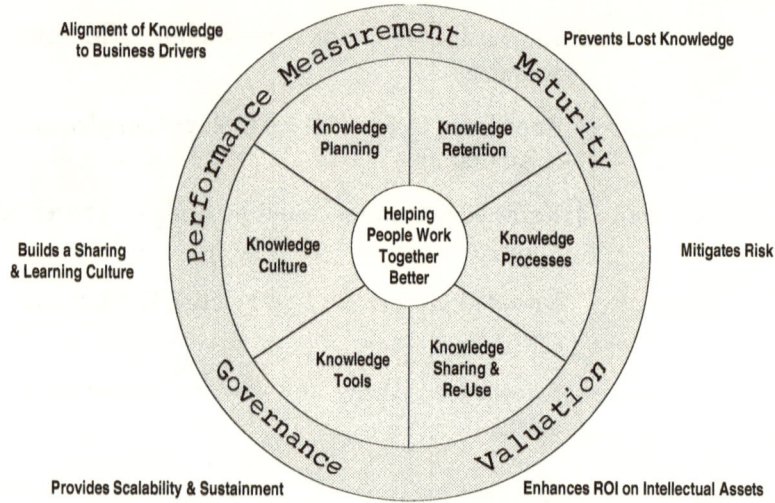

ILLUSTRATION 7: KM OBJECTIVES AND OUTCOMES

4.2.1. Knowledge planning

Organizations change structurally for many reasons. When designing and implementing organizational change, identification of unique and proprietary knowledge that might become crucial in the new organizational model is invaluable. It is also beneficial to identify general knowledge requirements, which can then be mapped into human-resource (HR) competencies. Finally, it is necessary to identify what new knowledge needs to be created to support the new organizational structure. KM routinely integrates this type of knowledge-planning analysis into organizational planning processes.

KM processes are a superset of business-management processes. To integrate knowledge requirements into process design, the KM diagnostic methodology is added to current business-process analysis methodologies when business analysts and management consultants are analyzing processes.

Business-process analysis typically traces the flow of information through its life cycle; KM, however, focuses on tracing the flow of knowledge through a decision-cycle. By combining these two forms of analysis, people and their tacit knowledge are integrated effectively into business-delivery systems.

4.2.2. Knowledge retention

Knowledge management is about people, their decision-making capabilities, and the knowledge they create, embody and use. As a key KM objective, knowledge management is embedded into HR management, planning, acquisition, development, sustainment, succession planning and separation. In each of these phases, knowledge-management process requirements are addressed from individual, team and organizational perspectives.

4.2.3. Knowledge tools

Most KM initiatives are enabled through effective use of information technology, governance, and process analysis. KM provides an ever-expanding suite of tools for the business-management toolbox. Determination of proper tool usage and process measures are outputs of the KM diagnostic methodology.

4.2.4. Knowledge culture

KM is also about building bridges between islands of knowledge. A bridge enables movement from one place to another; an island is a domain. An island may have its own culture, economy and values, and also an owner. Knowledge management recognizes that there is always a need for commerce between islands. Not everyone can know everything or make everything he or she needs to survive. KM provides a management vehicle to broker knowledge between different domains, establishing ownership and valuation, and implementing the necessary trade policies to allow knowledge transactions to take place.

Every organization has silos of knowledge. Today's intellectual-asset change agents force many organizations to realign knowledge horizontally to provide single-window access to clients, vendors and partners. These organizations are also trying to support internal employees by helping them find expert knowledge to offset the impact of an ageing workforce, with many senior managers eligible to retire.

The framework provides tools and processes to assist in the cultural adaptation and evolution of management of intellectual assets.

4.2.5. Knowledge processes

Organizational change agents are many and varied, and include economics, politics, markets, employee attrition, trends, fads and demographics. Organizations restructure to accommodate change agents, and in so doing often face a serious loss of key knowledge. The loss is due to improper understanding of people and the unique and/or proprietary knowledge they hold, and the degree to which the knowledge is crucial to the delivery of products and services. The severity of the knowledge loss can range from a brief interruption to complete organizational degradation. Whatever the magnitude of the loss, it's clear that change agents can generate the need to recreate lost knowledge at potentially significant cost.

To mitigate this risk, KM plays a new and valuable role by assessing the unique and proprietary knowledge requirements and assets associated with each discrete business problem/solution set. Knowing the importance of knowledge prior to realigning an organization enables efforts to be made to capture, reintegrate and find backup for these knowledge assets, and may also influence planning around organizational modeling.

A key KM objective is to integrate KM process analysis into current organizational models for performing business process analysis. Analyzing processes to optimize efficiencies and increase performance must include components of the human decision-making cycle, as these are crucial to the delivery of products and services. The framework's KM diagnostic methodology can be utilized as a guideline for extending classic business-process engineering.

4.2.6. Knowledge sharing and re-use

On both organizational and personal levels, massive financial investments are made in knowledge. To maximize return on investment in these intellectual assets, organizational and individual effectiveness at using and re-using knowledge must be managed and measured. The framework ensures that intellectual assets are effectively leveraged, and that application of lessons learned and best practices is enforced.

4.3.   KM Management Indices—Where are we now?

Six KM objectives exist within the framework. Each objective has been broken into six management indices for a total of 36 management indices.

Each index is inter-related with other indices through predefined weighted relationships. The result is a structured methodology to measure and manage the level of KM adoption and integration within organizations. Management-indices outputs are bound back to the KM objectives as a measure of maturity, and form the basis of the maturity assessment.

The 36 management indices are implemented as follows:

Objective 1: Knowledge planning—embedding KM into organizational planning

1. Progress implementing a governance model for KM?

2. Progress implementing a KM maturity model?

3. Progress implementing physical Centres of Expertise?

4. Progress implementing virtual Communities of Practice?

5. Progress organizing knowledge vertically?

6. Progress organizing knowledge horizontally?

Objective 2: Knowledge retention—embedding KM into human resources

7. Progress implementing KM into HR planning and management?

8. Progress implementing KM into HR succession planning?

9. Progress implementing KM into HR acquisition criteria?

10. Progress implementing KM into HR separation criteria?

11. Progress implementing KM into HR development criteria?

12. Progress implementing KM into HR sustainability criteria?

Objective 3: Knowledge tools—KM technologies, implementation and collaboration

13. Progress implementing decision matrices?

14. Progress implementing artificial-intelligence tools?

15. Progress implementing social-network analysis?

16. Progress implementing business-intelligence tools?

17. Progress implementing metadata-management tools?

18. Progress implementing collaborative-technology tools?

Objective 4: Knowledge culture—building bridges between islands of knowledge

19. Progress identifying knowledge domains?

20. Progress implementing knowledge policies?

21. Progress defining KM business drivers?

22. Progress identifying internal KM champions and stakeholders?

23. Progress defining how culture affects knowledge-management efforts?

24. Progress implementing KM rewards and recognition programs?

Objective 5: Knowledge processes—embedding KM into process engineering

25. Progress implementing a KM analysis process?

26. Progress embedding integrated feedback systems?

27. Progress implementing fast-lookup processes?

28. Progress implementing advanced research processes?

29. Progress embedding KM into people processes?

30. Progress embedding KM into technological processes?

Objective 6: Knowledge sharing and re-use—leveraging intellectual assets

31. Progress in formally advocating use and re-use of existing knowledge?

32. Progress implementing measurement and metrics for use and re-use of knowledge?

33. Progress managing intellectual property?

34. Progress managing best practices and lessons learned?

35. Progress formally tracking the quantity and quality of knowledge?

36. Progress implementing enforcement of use and re-use of knowledge?

4.3.1. Objective 1: Knowledge planning

1. Progress implementing a governance model for KM?

This index determines how far an organization has progressed in implementing a formal governance model to provide for the ongoing creation, sustainment, application, sharing, renewal and abandonment of intellectual assets within business units.

2. Progress implementing a KM maturity model?

This index determines how far an organization has progressed in implementing a KM maturity model that assesses the level of implementation of KM-related processes, people, technologies and content.

3. Progress implementing physical Centres of Expertise?

This index determines how far an organization has progressed in implementing Centres of Expertise that are physical in nature. Physical Centres of Expertise may include offices integrating subject-matter experts who focus on the support of internal staff and/or external clients.

4. Progress implementing virtual Communities of Practice?

This index determines how far an organization has progressed in implementing Communities of Practice, which provide a virtual workspace where staff members can collaborate with subject-matter experts, find documentation, capture lessons learned and best practices, and engage in open-forum discussions around a specific subject.

5. Progress organizing knowledge vertically?

This index determines how far an organization has progressed in organizing knowledge assets vertically to serve business units objectives. One example is Communities of Practice, which embed people from various levels and groups within a business unit for the purposes of facilitating delivery of the business unit's objectives. Vertical knowledge is primarily for the consumption and benefit of a specific business unit.

The opposite of this vertical organization is horizontal clustering of knowledge across multiple business units. A cluster may include external partners, where horizontal communities are established for cross-departmental or cross-business-unit specialists or for the sharing of knowledge that may not directly benefit the business unit, but may provide significant benefit to other business units or external interests.

6. Progress organizing knowledge horizontally?

This index determines how far an organization has progressed in organizing business units' knowledge assets horizontally, both internally and externally. Examples include horizontal clustering of knowledge across multiple business units. A cluster may include external partners, where horizontal communities are established for cross-departmental or cross-business-unit specialists or for the sharing of knowledge that may not directly benefit the business unit, but may provide significant benefit to other business units or external interests.

4.3.2. Objective 2: Knowledge retention

7. Progress implementing KM into HR planning and management?

This index determines how far an organization has progressed in implementing KM analysis and requirements into planning and management of human resources. Are training results, skills, certifications and competencies being tracked? Are KM criteria being integrated into the mapping of people to processes, teams and projects?

8. Progress implementing KM into HR succession planning?

This index determines how far an organization has progressed in implementing KM requirements into succession planning for human resources. Succession planning includes defining what unique knowledge, experience, mentoring and sharing skills are required in successors, defining roadmaps for mentoring successors, and engaging retired staff in knowledge transfer and communities of practice.

9. Progress implementing KM into HR acquisition criteria?

This index determines how far an organization has progressed in implementing KM requirements—including sharing skills, collaboration experience, team skills, mentoring experience—into the hiring process.

10. Progress implementing KM into HR separation criteria?

This index determines how far an organization has progressed in implementing KM requirements into separation processes. Is unique and proprietary knowledge being captured during exit?

11. Progress implementing KM into HR development criteria?

This index determines how far an organization has progressed in implementing KM requirements into ongoing development of human resources, including KM training, mentoring and advocacy.

12. Progress implementing KM into your HR sustainability criteria?

This index determines how far an organization has progressed in implementing KM requirements into ongoing support of human resources, including KM benefits at a personal level, and recognition, awards and compensation for knowledge sharing and mentoring.

4.3.3. Objective 3: Knowledge tools

13. Progress implementing decision matrices?

This index determines how far an organization has progressed in developing decision matrices that assist people through decision-making efforts within business units. Decision matrices contain lessons learned and best practices and help ensure that people ask the right questions.

14. Progress implementing artificial-intelligence tools?

This index determines how far an organization has progressed in developing artificial intelligence tools to assist decision-making efforts within business units.

15. Progress implementing social-network analysis?

This index determines how far an organization has progressed in performing social-network analysis. Social-network analysis maps who knows who, who knows what, who knows who knows what, who knows who knows who, and the people with whom employees collaborate on a regular basis to resolve discrete business problems.

16. Progress implementing business-intelligence tools?

This index determines how far an organization has progressed in developing business-intelligence tools—including data warehouses, CRM systems, and trending and analysis tools—to assist decision-making efforts within business units.

17. Progress implementing metadata-management tools?

This index determines how far an organization has progressed in integrating metadata-management tools to assist with categorizing and classifying codified knowledge within business units. Metadata is information about information.

18. Progress implementing collaborative technology tools?

This index determines how far an organization has progressed in integrating collaborative technologies into business units. Examples of collaborative technology tools include virtual communities of practice, discussion forums, video conferencing (desktop or meeting room), and shared project workspaces.

4.3.4. Objective 4: Knowledge culture

19. Progress identifying knowledge domains?

This index determines how far an organization has progressed in mapping where knowledge exists in relation to discrete business processes.

20. Progress implementing knowledge policies?

This index determines how far an organization has progressed in developing policies around the creation, sustainment, application, sharing, renewal and abandonment of knowledge in business units.

21. Progress defining KM business drivers?

This index determines how far an organization has progressed in identifying KM business drivers.

22. Progress identifying internal KM champions and stakeholders?

This index determines how far an organization has progressed in identifying KM champions and stakeholders for business units.

23. Progress defining how culture affects knowledge-management efforts?

This index determines how far an organization has progressed in identifying how a business unit's culture affects its ability to create, sustain, apply, share, renew and abandon knowledge.

24. Progress implementing KM rewards and recognition programs?

This index determines how far an organization has progressed in developing rewards and recognition programs related to knowledge creation, application, sharing, renewal and mentoring.

4.3.5. Objective 5: Knowledge processes

25. Progress implementing a KM analysis process?

This index determines how far an organization has progressed in implementing a framework for analyzing knowledge needs within each discrete business process and determining solution potentials. A KM analysis framework includes concepts, solution elements, and implementation processes.

26. Progress embedding integrated feedback systems?

This index determines how far an organization has progressed in implementing formal systems to capture what has been learned and feed it back into fast-lookup systems, such as trusted advisors or fast-lookup technologies.

27. Progress implementing fast-lookup processes?

This index determines how far an organization has progressed in implementing people and technology capable of providing fast answers to discrete business problems and solution sets. Examples of fast-lookup systems include individuals considered trusted advisors who are typically situated near the problem source, and fast-lookup technologies such as knowledge maps or frequently-asked-questions (FAQs) databases.

28. Progress implementing advanced research processes?

This index determines how far an organization has progressed in implementing advanced technologies such as taxonomies, business intelligence, artificial intelligence, data warehouses, and the inclusion of subject-matter experts (SMEs) who are dedicated to a discreet business problem and easily contacted.

29. Progress embedding KM into people processes?

This index determines how far an organization has progressed in implementing KM requirements into all business processes involving human interaction.

30. Progress embedding KM into technological processes?

This index determines how far an organization has progressed in implementing KM requirements into all business processes involving technology.

4.3.6. Objective 6: Knowledge sharing and re-use

31. Progress in formally advocating use and re-use of existing knowledge?

This index determines how far an organization has progressed in developing processes and management practices to advocate use and re-use of existing knowledge within business units.

32. Progress implementing measurement and metrics for use and re-use of knowledge?

This index determines how far an organization has progressed in developing measurements and metrics that monitor use and re-use of existing knowledge within business units.

33. Progress managing intellectual property?

This index determines how far an organization has progressed in developing management practices to deal with the creation, sustainment, application, sharing, renewal and abandonment of intellectual property, including policy development, legal processes and licensing.

34. Progress managing best practices and lessons learned?

This index determines how far an organization has progressed in developing management practices around creation, sustainment, application, sharing, renewal and abandonment of best practices and lessons learned.

35. Progress formally tracking the quantity and quality of knowledge?

This index determines how far an organization has progressed in developing systems and processes that track the quality and quantity of knowledge created by communities of practice, document repositories, knowledge bases, FAQs, discussion forums, and best-practice and lessons-learned repositories.

36. Progress implementing enforcement of use and re-use of knowledge?

This index determines how far an organization has progressed in developing enforcement practices to ensure use and re-use of existing knowledge within business units.

4.4. Frid Framework™ KM Maturity Assessment Levels

A Frid Framework™ KM maturity assessment produces a score that can be ranked against the following maturity levels:

4.4.1. Level 0—Knowledge chaotic

At this level, organizations should focus on:

1. Understanding and implementing the Frid Framework™ for Enterprise KM.

2. Advocating and adopting departmental KM vision and goals.

3. Performing a Frid Framework™ KM maturity assessment.

4.4.2. Level 1—Knowledge aware

At this level, organizations should focus on:

1. Understanding and implementing the Frid Framework™ for Enterprise KM.

2. Advocating and adopting departmental KM vision and goals.

3. Performing a Frid Framework™ KM maturity assessment.

4. Developing a KM roadmap.

5. Working collaboratively with the knowledge management office (KMO).

4.4.3. Level 2—Knowledge focused

At this level, organizations should focus on:

1. Understanding and implementing the Frid Framework™ for Enterprise KM.

2. Advocating and adopting departmental KM vision and goals.

3. Performing a Frid Framework™ KM maturity assessment.

4. Developing a KM roadmap.

5. Working collaboratively with the knowledge management office (KMO).

6. Embedding KM into process engineering.

7. Providing initial KM infrastructure, service and training.

8. Supporting early adopters and knowledge community.

9. Monitoring and reporting on management indices.

10. Including KM in budgets.

4.4.4. Level 3—Knowledge managed

At this level, organizations should focus on:

1. Understanding and implementing the Frid Framework™ for Enterprise KM.

2. Advocating and adopting departmental KM vision and goals.

3. Performing a Frid Framework™ KM maturity assessment.

4. Developing a KM roadmap.

5. Working collaboratively with the knowledge management office (KMO).

6. Embedding KM into process engineering.

7. Providing initial KM infrastructure, service and training.

8. Supporting early adopters and knowledge community.

9. Monitoring and reporting on management indices.

10. Including KM in budgets.

11. Embedding KM in performance reviews.

12. Embedding KM in business plans.

4.4.5. Level 4—Knowledge centric

At this level, organizations should focus on:

1. Understanding and implementing the Frid Framework™ for Enterprise KM.

2. Advocating and adopting departmental KM vision and goals.

3. Performing a Frid Framework™ KM maturity assessment.

4. Developing a KM roadmap.

5. Working collaboratively with the knowledge management office (KMO).

6. Embedding KM into process engineering.

7. Providing initial KM infrastructure, service and training.

8. Supporting early adopters and knowledge community.

9. Monitoring and reporting on management indices.

10. Including KM in budgets.

11. Embedding KM in performance reviews.

12. Embedding KM in business plans.

13. Institutionalizing successful initiatives.

14. Valuing intellectual assets.

5. THE FRID FRAMEWORK™ IMPLEMENTATION METHODOLOGY

The Frid Framework™ implementation methodology's stages and governance are depicted in the following illustration.

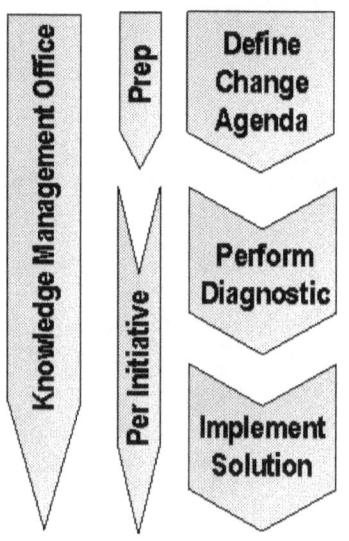

1. Maturity Model
2. Enterprise Roadmap
3. Toolbox

4. Champions & Stakeholders
5. Business Drivers
6. KM Analysis Process
7. Assessment & Determination

8. Advocate
9. Plan
10. Pilot
11. Implement
12. Institutionalize

ILLUSTRATION 8: THE FRID FRAMEWORK™ IMPLEMENTATION METHODOLOGY

5.1. The Knowledge Management Office (KMO)

One of the first steps to integrate knowledge management in a mid- to large-sized organization is establishment of a KMO to ensure proper governance. The KMO provides centralized alignment for KM initiatives across an enterprise. Illustration 9 outlines the KMO's key functions.

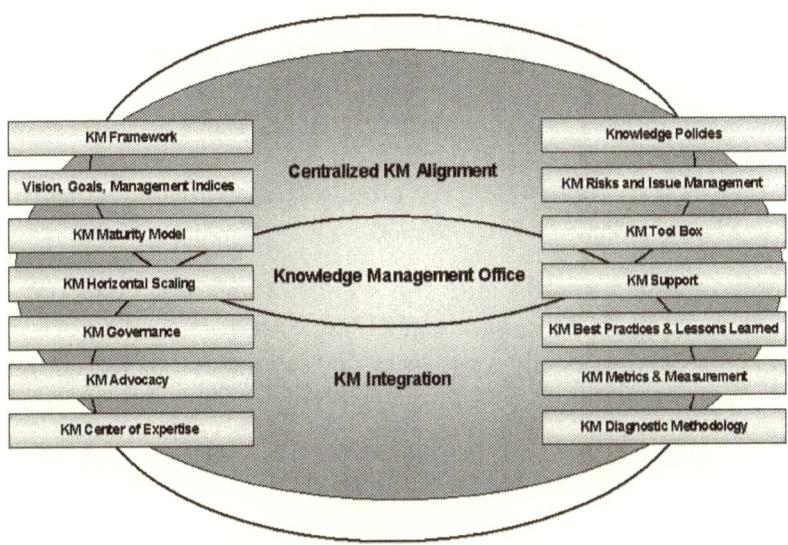

ILLUSTRATION 9: KNOWLEDGE MANAGEMENT OFFICE FUNCTIONS

A KMO's recommended staffing structure is demonstrated in Illustration 10.

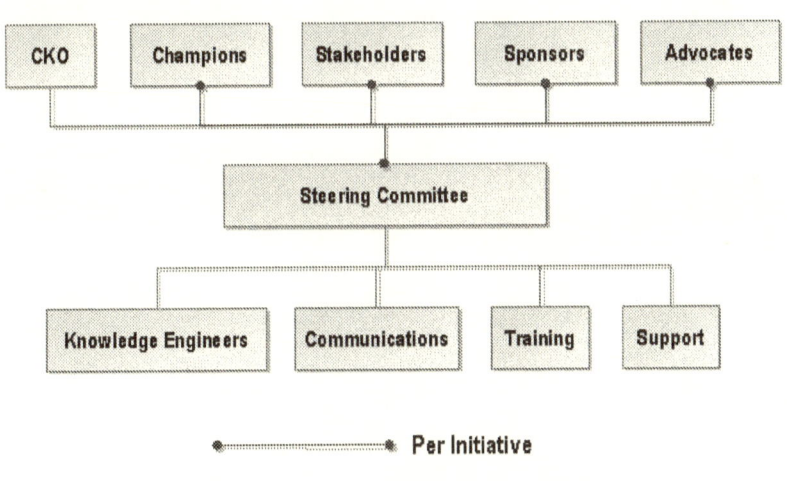

ILLUSTRATION 10: STAFFING THE KMO

Some staffing roles are permanent positions whereas others are specific to individual KM initiatives. The *Per Initiative* roles engage during the *perform diagnostic* and *implement solution* stages of the Frid Framework™ implementation methodology.

5.1.1. The Chief Knowledge Officer (CKO)

The Frid Framework™ for Enterprise KM defines the CKO as an authoritative role distinct from that of the Chief Information Officer (CIO). The CKO has unique characteristics and separate functionality from the CIO. Both CKO and CIO could reside with one individual or in a single office, but the differentiation of functions would still exist.

CKOs are concerned primarily with human and business decision cycles, and focused on management of and reporting on intellectual assets.

CIOs are concerned primarily with technology and information life cycles, and manage organizations explicit and transactional information and supporting technologies.

As shown in the following comparison table, the goals of both CKO and CIO are complementary.

This comparison table demonstrates how the CKO and CIO complement one another:

CKO	CIO
Psychological.	Physiological.
Owns and advocates organizational KM vision, goals and management indices.	Participates in implementation of organizational KM vision, goals and management indices.
Integrates KM into business plan.	Integrates KM into IM.
Analyzes decision cycles to evaluate how knowledge is created, valued and transferred throughout an organization.	Analyzes the IT lifecycle to evaluate how information is captured, created, stored, secured, shared and destroyed.
Analyzes information provided by CIO and categorizes and classifies it by defining taxonomies and knowledge maps.	Receives taxonomies and knowledge maps from CKO and uses them to codify information repositories.
Develops metadata standards.	Binds metadata to information.
Defines search, filter, relevancy and ranking requirements.	Implements search, filter, relevancy and ranking technologies.
Defines questions and relevancies.	Implements question matrices.
Defines how to engage knowledge silos and negotiate trade agreements between islands of knowledge.	Implements technologies that identify where knowledge silos exist and assists in brokering information.
Ensures KM is integrated into every workflow process.	Implements technological KM components of workflow.
Defines which people should work face-to-face, and when.	Implements technologies that enable face-to-face communications.
Advocates development and re-use of best practices.	Facilitates storage and retrieval of best practices.
Organizes real and virtual communities of practice.	Implements technologies that support communities of practice.
Defines business-intelligence requirements.	Implements business-intelligence technologies.
Identifies information repositories.	Manages access to information repositories.
Defines and implements KM incentive programs.	Implements measurement technologies to assess users' KM participation.

CKOs, for the most part, undertake roles of definition. Implementation is performed typically by the CIO for technological requirements and by senior and line managers for human aspects and advocacy.

The role of a CKO is perpetual. Times, people, processes and technologies change. 'Change management' changes also. A CKO is often the gatekeeper of change since knowledge managers understand that change is actually an underlying motivator in performance-enhancing organizations.

5.1.2. Champions and stakeholders

Champions and stakeholders are divided into two categories:

Enterprise KM Champions

⤷ **Organizational**

Per Initiative Champions & Stakeholders

⤷ **Operational**

5.1.3. Advocates and sponsors

Advocates and sponsors play crucial roles in the success or failure of knowledge-management initiatives. An advocate is usually someone respected in his or her field of expertise who is also willing to lead. A sponsor delivers funding.

Without advocates, knowledge-management initiatives are pointless. Without sponsors, there will be no funding.

It takes one or more advocates and at least one sponsor to build a community of practice (CoP). Typically, advocates are subject-matter experts who believe in the organizational value of the specific community; sponsors wish to solve a business problem and therefore deliver funding. Sponsors measure results; advocates measure quantity and quality. Organizations must recognize and reward advocates, and formalize the advocacy function into performance reviews.

One of the biggest obstacles to successful CoPs is stimulating desire to participate. The majority of individuals who belong to a community, be it social or virtual, prefer to be bystanders. Many people prefer not to broadcast information to other individuals, let alone to an entire community, for fear they will be seen to not know something, or that what they know is incorrect. Employees need to feel confident that they will not be publicly humiliated in a CoP.

For this reason, an advocate plays an extremely important role. The advocate usually leads the first round of discussions, and delivers open and honest questions and responses that do not belittle CoP members. Being a subject-matter expert in the CoP topic, an advocate encourages others to discuss related matters that arise outside of the CoP. Such open, non-judgmental discussion generates exponential growth within the CoP for a period of time—typically over three to six months. Change happens slowly; employees will not adopt new technology just because a new icon appears on their desktops. Should expected growth not occur, inappropriate advocates may be the reason.

Initially, CoP members sample the value of content flowing through a community, and then begin to post low-risk questions to test feedback. The advocate encourages other subject-matter experts to post detailed and supportive responses to members' questions. The first round of responses sets the quality, level of professional courtesy, and expected due diligence of future replies. As the CoP becomes more widespread, growth is significant and the advocate recruit additional advocates and subject-matter experts who are expected to abide by established ground rules.

A second stage occurs when the CoP begins to assimilate a wealth of knowledge, which is monitored by advocates for redundancy. Advocates must also constantly educate community users to search for historical questions, documents, issues and risks that may have previously addressed an issue. CoP members who see the same questions being asked repeatedly get tired of the repetition and begin to lose interest in the community. Not measuring for redundancy means a growing problem is being missed, and that advantage is not being taken of intellectual assets already present. Re-use of existing knowledge is a large part of the return on investment delivered by communities of practice.

Moderated discussions control redundancy and provide clues to the health of a community. The drawback to moderated communities is the time delay caused by advocates having to moderate and research posted issues. In today's instant society, people prefer fast information to best information. If use of the CoP declines, the management team (CKO, governance, sponsor and advocates) needs to find out why. Does it take too much time to access information from the CoP? Are search capabilities too weak and confusing? Do users need additional training?

A harmonious balance among delivering fast information, providing quality information, and re-using intellectual assets should be encapsulated by the CKO, sponsors, advocates, steering committee and governance board when defining initial CoP roles and responsibilities.

5.1.4. Steering committees and governance

Undertaking a KM initiative for all but the smallest of projects typically requires establishment of a steering committee for the lifecycle of the project. Following implementation, ongoing guidance of the KM program comes through governance.

Many KM initiatives span multiple functions, departments and agencies. It is necessary, therefore, to strive continually to achieve buy-in from all levels and employees that the initiative will impact. Building a cross-functional steering committee is a desired first-step to build consensus across the KM domain of influence.

Efforts spent building a KM steering committee often deliver great long-term benefits; an effective steering committee opens dialog on many concerns. For this reason, members of the steering committee should be chosen with great care, with each member being a respected spokesperson of the line of business he or she represents. Steering committee members do not need to be technically inclined. The CKO, however, should have a strong grasp of technical issues to ensure that technical questions are addressed from a high-level business perspective and weighed into overall strategy.

Unlike the steering committee, which is designed to guide design and implementation of the KM initiative and is primarily staffed with line-of-business representatives, a governance board should be comprised of advocates, sponsors and stakeholders. Governance board size is not as important as the breadth and depth of representation. The governance board must ensure that KM program goals are met, and realign goals or terminate the program based on defined abandonment metrics. The governance board is responsible to the KM program's sponsors and members alike, and works to ensure an ongoing funding model.

5.1.5. Knowledge engineers

Knowledge engineers are business analysts trained in the Frid Framework™ KM analysis process. Traditional business-analysis functions track flow of information throughout a transaction lifecycle; knowledge engineers use the Frid Framework™ KM analysis process to track flow of knowledge and intellectual assets through a decision cycle.

5.1.6. Communications

Communications are an essential component of design and deployment of a successful KM program. Communicating awareness of the KM project is paramount in the re-use of intellectual capital. If employees do not know that knowledge and information exist, and more importantly where knowledge and information can be found, it will not get used. Awareness can be built through many communications vehicles including focus groups, workshops, and electronic and hardcopy project updates, information sheets and newsletters.

Messages from senior executives demonstrate that a KM program is sanctioned from the top. Regular communications from users' direct management team enforce the message of collaboration, consensus and agreement. Messages should be unambiguous and concise, and clearly indicate what users gain from the initiative. This last communication is a key motivator to participation, the importance of which cannot be understated. If employees are not told, many times and in many different ways, what they stand to gain, active participants will be few and far between.

The communications team or individual should conduct interviews regularly throughout the lifecycle of the initiative to find out if the value system and culture within the initiative are changing for better or worse. This feedback should be discussed at every governance board meeting.

The communications team:

1. Finds out what clients want.

2. Repackages messages in a client-friendly manner.

3. Sells an initiative to clients once it's up and running.

4. Continues ongoing promotion of the initiative's merits.

5. Collects initiative feedback, searching for ways to improve the initiative.

6. Promotes new features and enhancements.

A communications plan should be developed and become an integral part of every KM initiative.

5.1.7. Training

As with the deployment of any new initiative, training is crucial. KM training takes two forms awareness training and user training.

KM awareness training is targeted primarily at advocates. Awareness training helps advocates learn:

1. what motivates individuals to participate;

2. how to encourage participation;

3. how to measure and monitor quality and quantity;

4. how to watch for redundancy;

5. how to coach for re-use of information;

6. how to monitor the social courtesies within a community; and

7. how to identify and engage other advocates.

KM awareness training, however, is not limited to advocates; it is also required for other KM aspects and tools. Employees need to be made aware of other KM initiatives such as knowledge maps, directories, business intelligence, and many other information repositories. Information overload is a KM killer, and proliferation of too many KM tools stretches employees' patience. Trainers and knowledge engineers must look for overlap and consistency of approach to minimize user impact and maximize participation.

A formal KM awareness program should be incorporated into the overall organizational training mandate to ensure information about knowledge management is crystallized and synchronized throughout all training programs.

KM user training deals with the processes surrounding implementation of the KM program and associated technologies. Trainers should look proactively for regular feedback from advocates and sponsors of every KM initiative. This feedback identifies silos in need of cultivation (not participating), and employees in need of additional training because they are trying to bypass a process or cannot see value in participation.

5.2. Change agents and the management of change

Knowledge management is one of the new weapons in the battle to manage change. Change management and the management of change are not new concepts. The tools embodied within the Frid Framework™ for Enterprise KM enable a controlled approach to analyzing the impact of intellectual-asset change agents and help build strategies to promote and implement managed change. The framework targets change agents that affect intellectual assets.

Change agents can be many and varied. For example, the Government of Canada (GoC) has several priority change agents that, unless managed effectively, will negatively impact service delivery over the long-term:

- **Knowledge attrition:** 70 percent of GoC senior executives are approaching retirement, with few experienced employees available to replace them. Employees who could be promoted to replace retiring executives are in the same age range.

- **Modern comptrollership:** a government-wide management initiative focused on sound resource management and effective decision-making. The initiative goes beyond financial control and accounting, involving all departmental employees and necessitating fundamental change in the corporate culture of the public service.

- **Citizens' empowerment:** a better-informed public demands simple, single-window access, greater self-service, and easier direct access to government services.

Understanding which change agents are likely to affect intellectual assets enables management to establish a change agenda, which mitigates risk by managing the change effectively.

5.2.1. GoC internal change agents

The GoC faces a unique problem over the next five to ten years: 70 percent of senior executives are approaching retirement, and there are few experienced employees to replace them. Employees who could be promoted to replace retiring executives are in the same age range.

The bulk of the intellectual capital that resides in the minds of these retiring executives will leave with them, creating a knowledge vacuum that could cripple public services seriously.

Studies have also shown a trend of short-term hiring in the GoC. Short-term hiring generally leads to an inexperienced workforce with little or no understanding of internal and external organizational relationships, and few political skills.

In a 2001 report, the Office of the Auditor General of Canada stated:

> **Pressures that contribute to "human capital" challenges**
>
> The public service faces a significant "human capital" challenge—the need for enough skilled people to perform its work. The Clerk of the Privy Council has identified three human resource priorities across the public service to address the challenge: recruitment (hiring new staff to the public service), retention (keeping competent staff), and learning (developing staff to ensure the continuing competency of the public service).
>
> The key factors that affect recruitment today are demographics inside the public service; a shift in the nature of the work, requiring staff who are more highly skilled and more educated; an increasingly tight labour force that will be in more demand than it can supply; and the negative perceptions of the public service as a career choice.
>
> Demographics. In December 2000, the Auditor General of Canada reported that 75 percent of public service executives would be eligible to retire without penalty by 2008. A survey of executives and equivalents, undertaken in 2001 by the Association of Professional Executives of the Public Service of Canada (APEX) and Ekos Research Associates Inc., found that 40 percent actually plan to retire in the next five years, and an additional 35 percent in the next

six to ten years. Employees who could replace them, those at levels just below Executive ranks who have the necessary qualifications, have a similar age profile.

At the same time, youth are underrepresented in the public service, as a result of limited hiring by the government in the period of Program Review. The proportion of employees who are under the age of 35 is about half as big in the public service as in the general workforce.

Shifting nature of work. *The nature of work in the federal public service has shifted. The decision to delegate many operational functions to outside organizations and the increasing computerization of work have reduced the number of operational and support staff. Computerization, globalization, and an increasingly complex working environment call for higher levels of skills; more positions in the public service now require post-secondary education.*

Labour force. *As the Auditor General of Canada reported in April 1998, the youth population is decreasing; by 2010, the retiring population will outnumber youth, creating conditions for major labour shortages. Private sector firms already talk about a "war for talent." Every day, newspapers predict a shortage of candidates for professional and skilled employment.*

Career choice. *Finally, the public service has an image problem. A 1999 employee survey in the federal public service and some academic studies, such as Career Development in the Federal Public Service: Building a World-Class Workforce, have underlined some of the problems in the workplace. Surveys of university students by the Public Service Commission have confirmed that they do not consider the public service as desirable a place to work as students once did.*

In November 2001, after years of research and consultation, the Association of Professional Executives of the Public Service of Canada (APEX) published *Reforming Human Resources Management in the Public Service of Canada* . The report can be summed up briefly:

"Only meaningful, profound change in the management of people will enable the Public Service of Canada to remain relevant and effective for the 21st century."

Results of APEX's 2001 *Executive Cadre Retention and Transition Planning Survey* show that:

"Our capacity to keep people is dependent on our ability to make work meaningful and challenging and to foster a climate for professional learning and growth."

From the above reports, it is obvious that a short- and long-term need exists for government agencies to identify, transfer and capture the tacit knowledge—such as experience, relationships, best practices and lessons learned—that resides at the executive level of Canadian government. Senior executives are typically senior because of the wealth of personal experience they command. In a normal mentoring environment this knowledge would be cultivated and bestowed on junior individuals over the course of many years. With fewer junior-level individuals in the system, and a trend of short-term hiring, much of this knowledge is disappearing with retiring employees, leaving new promotees with insufficient skills to meet the demands of their new jobs.

Knowledge-management practices help leverage and manage intellectual assets in a way that assists organizations to achieve their objectives. KM also assists in identifying subject-matter experts and systems that possess relevant information. KM provides the means to connect and communicate with these resources, and to map knowledge directly to business processes and drivers.

KM will become a predominant issue throughout the Government of Canada over the next few years. However, because KM is about building additional functionality into standard business-management practices, migration should be organic.

5.2.2. GoC external change agents

Citizens, global economics and information technology place ever increasing demands on current government programs and systems. Changes in any of these factors affect the way Canadian public services are created, delivered and maintained.

From *The APEX Perspective Reform of Human Resources Management*:

> *Change within the Public Service is being driven at least partially by a number of outside forces. These are:*
>
> *Globalization: More than a purely economic phenomenon, social policy too is made in a global context and in conjunction with other states.*
>
> *Information technology: Citizen demands for more accessible and efficient services are driving the technology revolution in all levels of government and in business.*
>
> *Empowerment of citizens: A better-informed public demands single window access, greater self-service, and easier direct access to government services. It wants to see better cooperation between departments and different levels of government, as well as closer collaboration with other sectors: public, non-profit, voluntary. Citizens also want to have greater influence on decision-making.*
>
> *Stewardship: There is increased pressure for responsible spending, due diligence and horizontal management of key issues, such as the environment.*

External motivators are key drivers of knowledge-management initiatives. KM delivers an understanding of what knowledge is available, what knowledge is missing, who or what has the knowledge, how it can be found, how people want to view it, how it is classified and categorized, how valuable it is, and how one piece of knowledge may be related to others. These functions combine to provide cross-functional access to information for Canadian citizens.

Citizens can be classified into various audiences including business, educational and legal. KM recognizes that each audience has different needs and perspectives when accessing and applying information. Each audience will have preferences about how information is viewed, classified, categorized and organized; no single methodology provides a utopian model. Therefore, multiple views (dimensions) must be built into information. Each view must be customized to satisfy the specific needs of the intended audience.

For example, a research scientist may want information on current Alzheimer's disease research efforts. The scientist will want to search though government information banks primarily within the health sector for information specifically relating to Alzheimer's research. On the other hand, a citizen whose parent may have Alzheimer's will more likely approach the same body of information by asking life questions such as: What government services are available to help someone with Alzheimer's? These individuals will want information from all sectors with Alzheimer's support programs and information.

The unique multilingual aspects of Canadian government must also be considered when planning any KM program. Knowledge can exist in multiple languages and should be made available in the language of the users choice. However, interpretation of knowledge across languages can be time consuming and expensive. Both knowledge conversion and collaboration across multiple languages present barriers most technologies and single-language countries do not have to overcome.

5.2.3. Scientific change creation

A further advantage to implementing knowledge management is change creation.

Knowledge is the one common denominator that all individuals interact with on a daily basis. Knowledge is required at every organizational level for employees to make decisions and to execute tasks; individuals require knowledge if they are to grow.

In 1927, Elton Mayo carried out an experiment, called the Hawthorne experiment, at the Western Electric Company in Illinois. Mayo hoped to discover optimum levels of plant illumination and proper timing of rest periods by experimenting with selected groups of workers. He discovered that it did not matter how the workers' environment was altered; merely being chosen for an experiment improved productivity—the so-called Hawthorne effect.

Mayo realized that the experiment's significant variable was not physiological but psychological. A series of experiments was performed, involving assembly of telephone relays; test and control groups were subjected to changes in wages, rest periods, workweeks, temperature, humidity and other factors. Output continued to increase no matter how physical conditions were varied; indeed, even when conditions were returned to initial levels, productivity remained 25 percent above its original value. Mayo concluded that the reason lay in workers' attitudes toward their jobs and the company. Merely by asking employees' cooperation in the test, investigators had stimulated a new attitude among employees, who now felt themselves part of an important group whose help and advice were being sought by the company.

Sponsorship of knowledge management potentially involves everyone in an enterprise, and introduces positive change, because KM's primary role is to help people work together more effectively. The Hawthorne experiment indicates that this change, which is psychological in nature, will help create a new workplace attitude. The new attitude helps to increase productivity. KM lends itself well to creating enterprise-wide positive change.

5.3. Change agenda: common KM infrastructure

Within the Frid Framework™ for Enterprise KM, a change agenda is developed to address change agents. A maturity model, roadmap and toolbox are infrastructure components recommended to be in place before the start of specific KM implementations:

5.3.1. Maturity model

Implementation of a KM maturity model and establishment of an initial KM baseline are the second step in the change agenda. The baseline can be referred to at regular intervals to measure progress of implementation. Refer to section 4.3: *KM Management Indices—Where are we now?*

5.3.2. Roadmap

Establishment of an enterprise roadmap and, if necessary, additional roadmaps for sub-entities within the organization are a required third step in the change agenda. The lowest level of granularity recommended for development of roadmaps is the discrete business unit.

Stage 1 Initiate	Stage 2 Mobilize	Stage 3 Institutionalize	Stage 4 Innovate
▪ Adopt KM Framework ▪ Define Roadmap ▪ Perform Maturity Assessment ▪ Advocate Results ▪ Establish KMO ▪ Provide Initial infrastructure, service and training ▪ Support the early adopters	▪ Develop & implement KM road maps in the business units ▪ Provide KM Analysis, service and training ▪ Provide centralized support for business unit Knowledge Engineers ▪ Integrate KM in the business processes	▪ Integrate KM in the performance reviews ▪ Integrate KM into organizational business plan ▪ Develop Cross-Departmental KM Roadmap	▪ Promote new knowledge based service offerings ▪ Establish knowledge sharing and creation as career criteria ▪ Implement intelligent KM workplaces ▪ Focus innovation

ILLUSTRATION 11: ENTERPRISE KM ROADMAP—BASED ON SIEMENS CORP. ROADMAP STAGES

5.3.3. Toolbox

Establishment of a centralized toolbox, managed by the KMO, for employees across an organization to access is the fourth step in the change agenda. At a minimum, the toolbox should contain:

- a KM framework guide, such as the Frid Framework™ for Enterprise KM;

- KM policies;

- a KM maturity model;

- a KM analysis process;

- KM best practices;

- KM lessons learned;

- a KM discussion forum;

- a KM document repository;

- KM contacts;

- KM risk-, issue- and opportunity-management tools;

- KM links;

- KM guides and training materials;

- KM templates; and

- KM presentation materials.

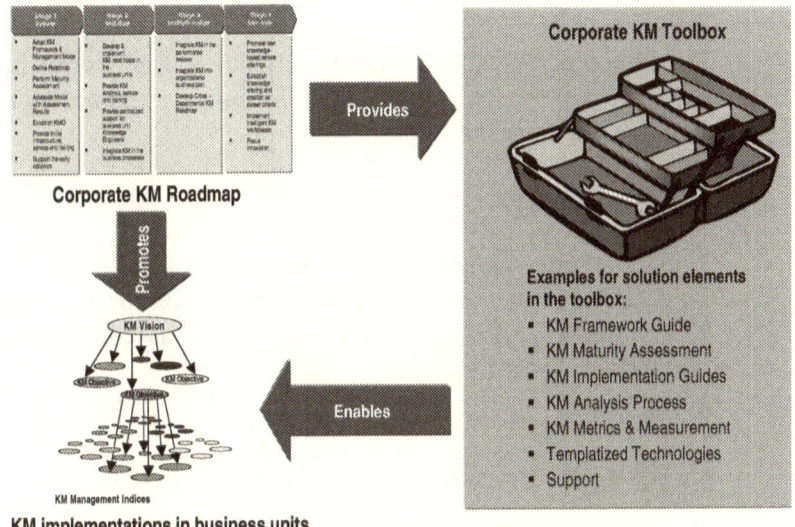

ILLUSTRATION 12: KM TOOLBOX INTEGRATION

5.4.   Perform diagnostics for individual KM initiatives

To this point, efforts have been concentrated on building infrastructure to support a KM initiative. However, once change agents have been analyzed and a change agenda defined, an enterprise is ready to undertake individual KM initiatives.

The *Perform diagnostics and implement solutions* stage is unique for each KM initiative.

The Frid Framework™ is optimized to accommodate KM initiatives in a single business unit and to focus on a discrete business process (problem/solution set). Typically, a single business unit encapsulates a single knowledge domain and has immediate demands for vertical knowledge clustering to meet business-unit objectives. The framework also accommodates demands for horizontal knowledge clustering that stem from the need to buy, sell or broker knowledge across multiple business units, knowledge domains, external trading partners, and clients.

Most KM initiatives start within a single business unit, because the KM analysis process targets discrete business problem/solution sets, and business problems are generally more apparent in tactical areas. However, some KM analysis-process outcomes may require horizontal integration across multiple business units, knowledge domains, external trading partners, and clients even though the process originated within a single business unit.

5.4.1. Business drivers

Knowledge management is really *knowledge-enabled business management*. There must, therefore, be a business reason for undertaking any KM initiative, and the business reason must have something to do with achieving business goals.

Questions that need to be answered include:

1. What is the business problem that needs to be solved?

2. What knowledge-based assets are involved?

3. How do are these assets identified, valued, created, improved, protected and abandoned?

A business problem to which KM analysis can offer significant value might demonstrate one or more of the following characteristics:

- A loss of people, which will affect the capability of an organization, department, sector or branch to complete its mission.

- A lack of efficiency, which is consuming resources and not achieving desired goals.

- An inability of an organization or department to meet commitments.

- A vision or goal that needs realignment.

When the business driver has been identified, it must be accompanied by a fixed measuring device so that return on investment can be clearly demonstrated. If an end goal is identified prior to the start of an initiative, outcomes are easily measured and quantifiable to everyone.

For example, when attempting to convince business-unit managers of the merits of knowledge management, they might indicate that an improvement in customer satisfaction is a business necessity. To further define the problem, the following questions need to be asked:

1. How is customer satisfaction or dissatisfaction measured at the present time?

2. What level of satisfaction is currently being achieved?

3. By what process is customer satisfaction determined?

4. At what point will the organization accept that customers are satisfied?

5. How much time is available to achieve the desired level of satisfaction?

Armed with this level of detail, the Frid Framework™ KM diagnostic methodology can be implemented. Existing processes can then be analyzed, and problems associated with intellectual assets and human decision-making that might play a role in customer dissatisfaction can be discovered. An assessment and determination process can be performed to produce recommendations based on predetermined success metrics.

5.4.2. Champions and stakeholders

As with most undertakings in the business world, champions are necessary to sponsor the KM cause, proclaim it to executives, and provide and attract funding.

The output of the KM analysis process is a KM discovery report, which articulates the problem(s). The report provides champions with the information necessary to secure the next round of funding, which will produce a report called the KM recommendations report. The recommendations report analyzes potential solutions and the parameters they impose. From this report, champions and stakeholders determine what approach (if any) they are willing to undertake, and acquire sufficient information to substantiate an application for the funding required to implement recommended solution(s).

Champions also help to identify stakeholders. Stakeholders are those individuals or groups that receive direct—and sometimes indirect—benefits from a KM initiative; they are also the individuals or groups that may be directly—and sometimes indirectly—affected.

5.4.3. Project charter: sample table of contents

5.4.3.1.   Project overview

- Project purpose

- Project scope

- Project objectives

- Outstanding issues

- Approvals

- References

- Terminology

5.4.3.2.   Project approach

- Project deliverables and quality objectives

- Organization, responsibilities and project organization chart

- Dependencies

- Plans for support activities:

    - Project training

    - Technical reviews

    - Documentation support

    - Status monitoring

    - Communications plan (see next section)

- Contract and procurement management

- Project facilities and resource requirements

- Risk management

- Process options and deviations

- Stages

- Project control

- Project-management tools
- Risk, opportunity, issue and change management
- Activity reports
- Team-leader meetings
- Project meetings
- Project progress reports

- Quality control activities

- Project schedule

- Project effort estimate

- Project cost estimate

- Appendices

5.4.3.3.   Document change control

A project charter should also contain some type of document-version-control table similar to the following:

Version #	Date of Issue	Author(s)	Brief Description of Change
1.0	22 Dec 2001	G. Zilla	Preliminary draft to facilitate planning and information collection
1.1	15 Jan 2002	J. Daniels	Draft for consultation with project sponsor and ABC officials

ILLUSTRATION 13: DOCUMENT CHANGE CONTROL TABLE

5.4.4. KM initiative lifecycle

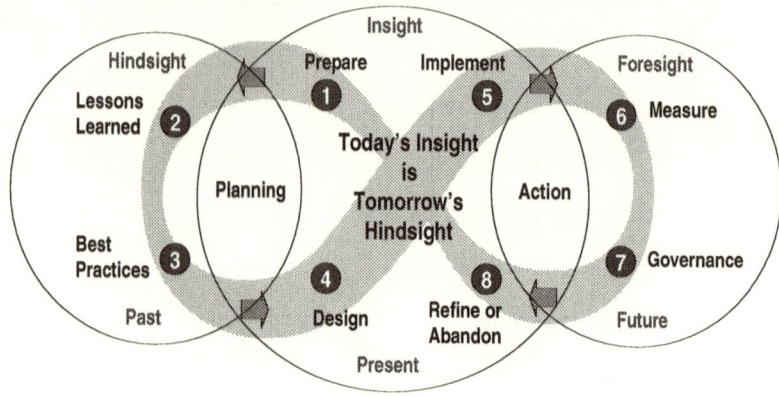

ILLUSTRATION 14: KM INITIATIVE LIFECYCLE

The KM initiative lifecycle is a progressive loop, constantly moving forward in time. The lifecycle provides an entrance at Step 1—Preparation and a planned abandonment strategy in Step 8—Refine or abandon.

Step 1—Prepare (What's wrong?)

Implementation of the Frid Framework™ KM analysis process.

Step 2—Lessons learned (What shouldn't we do?)

Implementation of the Frid Framework™ KM assessment and determination, and input of historical lessons learned.

Step 3—Best practices (What should we do?)

Continued implementation of the Frid Framework™ KM assessment and determination, and input of recommended best practices.

Step 4—Design (Why should we do it?)

Continued implementation of the Frid Framework™ KM assessment and determination, and generation of recommendations.

Step 5—Implement (How should we do it?)

Implementation of the Frid Framework™ KM initiative roadmap.

Step 6—Measure (How well did we do?)

Measure outcomes and assess them against projected outcomes defined in earlier stages.

Step 7—Governance (Where do we go from here?)

Make management decisions, report on the health of the initiative, and provide:

- funding and approval for further growth and refinements;
- funding and approval for corrective measures; or
- approval for strategic abandonment.

Step 8—Refine or abandon (How do we get there?)

In step eight the initiative either follows the predestined course set by the governance body, moves back into planning for improvements or growth, or is shut down in an an organized fashion (planned abandonment).

5.4.5. Critical Success factors

- KM acknowledges knowledge domains and ownership.
- KM targets discrete business problems (problem/solution sets).
- KM requires advocacy and enforcement.
- KM must be integrated into workflow.
- Users see a personal benefit in participation.
- KM requires committed sponsorship and on-going management.

5.4.6. Why KM initiatives fail: survey statistics

20 %: lack of user uptake due to lack of communication.

19 %: failure to integrate KM into everyday workflow processes.

18 %: lack of time or too complicated to learn.

15 %: lack of training.

13 %: users don't see personal benefits.

7 %: senior management did not fully support the KM initiative.

7 %: technical problems.

5.4.7. KM initiative roadmap

The five phases outlined in the KM initiative roadmap can be adapted to any formal project-management framework, such as MSF or RUP, on which an organization has standardized.

ILLUSTRATION 15: KM INITIATIVE ROADMAP STAGES

5.4.8. Phase 1: Advocacy

Advocacy at the beginning of a KM initiative formalizes communications and builds consensus. Without effective advocacy, failure rates are high. Refer to crucial success factors above.

5.4.9. Phase 2: Planning

As with any project, a reasonable percentage of budget and time should be spent planning.

Projects should also be detailed on paper. Documentation of every step of an initiative is vital; these records will become organizational best practices. Recording progress on paper also enables others to provide insight that might save time and money.

Refer to section 5.4.3: *Project charter: sample table of contents*

A change-management framework should be used to ensure the scope of the project doesn't change and consume more funds than those allocated.

If time and budget allow, an external advisor should perform a gap analysis toward the end of the planning phase. The analysis can be a simple document that outlines:

1. what the vision is;

2. where the organization is now; and

3. what needs to be done to enable the organization to reach its vision goals.

An independent gap analysis also enables executives and initiative advocates to feel confident about requesting and contributing further funding.

5.4.10. Phase 3: Piloting

Depending on the special nature of the KM program, implementation relies on many things including:

1. funding;

2. timing;

3. technology issues;

4. human resources;

5. training;

6. operations;

7. communications; and

8. support.

At this phase, organizations should be utilizing a formal project-management framework that incorporates project phases, communications, controls, templates and tools. Project-management frameworks lend great credibility to projects, providing timelines, milestones and deliverables that are quantifiable for everyone involved. Numerous technological project-management systems are available, and all provide a suite of formal processes, which initially can appear overwhelming. However, organizations can use only those processes they really need.

At the end of the piloting phase, the KM initiative is deployed to a select group of early adopters who will provide feedback to the development team.

5.4.11. Phase 4: Implementation

In phase four, the KM program moves into production in a selective fashion. Core development-team members—those who developed the technological components—are no longer the program support system, although they may still help on an occasional basis to assist transition. Processes have been turned over to management, and technological systems to operations teams, to manage and maintain. The training department has training requirements and materials developed into formal programs, and support infrastructure is in place.

At this stage, the program is in operation in a select area of the organization, user confidence is gained, the initiative is modified as necessary, and results are measured.

Phase four should see the KM initiative being integrated into daily workflow. If the initiative is not integrated successfully, it will likely die. The knowledge engineers' and advocates' jobs are not complete until successful workflow integration occurs.

5.4.12. Phase 5: Institutionalization

If phase four results prove the KM initiative worthy of further expansion, phase five sees the KMO extending the successful program across the enterprise.

The initiative is adopted into the organizational business plan, aspects of the program are integrated into employee performance reviews, and it is recognized as an integral component of organizational success.

If a tactical solution is being deployed, it may never be institutionalized fully; however, this is not necessarily a problem. Many tactical programs are successful without becoming organizational cornerstones.

A KM initiative is successful if it produces the desired outcomes.

5.4.13. KM analysis process

Refer to Section 6: *Frid Framework™ KM Diagnostic Methodology*.

5.4.14. Assessment and determination

Refer to Section 6: *Frid Framework™ KM Diagnostic Methodology*.

6. FRID FRAMEWORK™ KM DIAGNOSTIC METHODOLOGY

6.1. Introduction

The Frid Framework™ KM diagnostic methodology encapsulates two functions:

- analysis process; and
- assessment and determination.

6.2. Analysis Process

The first aspect of the diagnostic methodology is the analysis process, which identifies and reports on various aspects of the knowledge required and utilized throughout a discrete business problem/solution set. The output of the analysis process is a KM discovery report, a document that describes the nature of the problem(s).

Depending on scope, the report study should take one or two people to perform the initial analysis two to four weeks.

The methodology then divides the requirements—obtained as outputs of the KM analysis process—into a solution matrix. The matrix is divided into the people, processes, technology and content required to address a solution strategy. Each element of the matrix is evaluated against the requirements and multiple environmental factors. The output of the solution matrix is a KM recommendations report.

Discovery report

The analysis process divides the various facets of decision making within the problem/solution set to identify:

1. the nature of the problem and the preferred solution;

2. the profile-type and requirements of the user performing the research;

3. the knowledge needed by researchers;

4. whether the required knowledge is unique, common, or needs to be created;

5. the people, processes and tools necessary to locate the knowledge;

6. whether available knowledge is understandable to researchers;

7. how best to capture and codify new knowledge upon successful research outcome;

8. the repair process to follow in the event of unsuccessful outcome;

9. how to improve people, processes and tools based on research outcomes;

10. knowledge-based risks, issues and opportunities;

11. sharing, sustainment, renewal, abandonment and succession requirements; and

12. the estimated financial value associated with unique knowledge components.

Illustration 16 outlines the components of the analysis processes used within the Frid Framework™ for Enterprise KM:

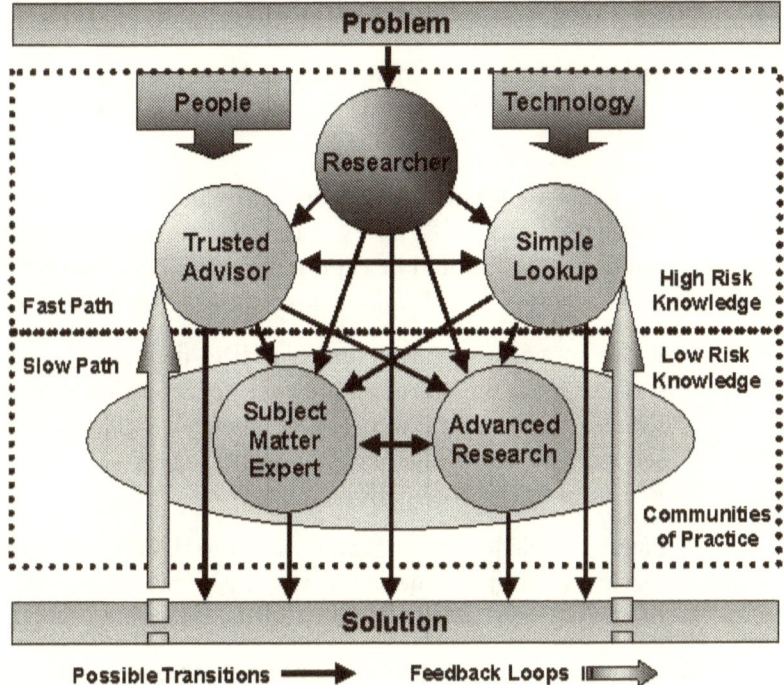

ILLUSTRATION 16: KM ANALYSIS PROCESS—DISCOVERY

6.2.1. The problem/solution approach

The first step in performing KM analysis is to identify a problem. The problem should be a discrete business problem and, at a minimum, must demonstrate one or more of the following characteristics:

- loss of people, which will affect the ability of the organization, department or business unit to complete its mission;

- lack of efficiency that consumes resources and fails to achieve desired goals;

- inability of the organization, department or business unit to meet its commitments; and

- vision or goals in need of realignment.

6.2.2. Knowledge types and risk analysis

KM analysis focuses on identifying and categorizing process-crucial knowledge. Identification and categorization can be achieved through asking and answering three questions:

1. Is the knowledge unique or proprietary, and crucial to delivery of a product or service? If all these criteria are met, the knowledge is important and should be captured, codified and valued. It should also be flagged as a *High Level Risk* until captured and codified.

2. Is the knowledge general, and crucial to delivery of a product or service? If all these criteria are met, the knowledge requirement should be integrated into HR competencies for the product or service. The knowledge should also be flagged as a *Medium Level Risk* until integrated in HR competencies.

3. Is the knowledge missing, and crucial to delivery of a product or service? If all these criteria are met, the knowledge should be identified as a *High Level Issue* that requires resolution.

Throughout the analysis process, a high probability exists that large volumes of general knowledge not necessarily crucial to the delivery of products and services will be revealed. The analysis process, however, focuses specifically on knowledge crucial to delivery of a product or service.

6.2.3. The researcher profile

The researcher profile describes the nature and requirements of the user attempting to find information. Profiles include:

1. External researcher

    An individual outside an organization who wishes to work independently. External researchers can belong to one of five groups:

    • business;

    • government;

    • education;

    • citizen; and

    • client.

Each of the above groups will typically have a different set of requirements and require different navigation structures to search for information. Each group thinks about a business problem/solution set differently. By attempting to identify to which group a researcher belongs at the beginning of the KM process, access can be provided to required information in a manner that accommodates the researcher's individual way of thinking, searching and categorizing.

2.   **Internal researcher**

An individual inside an organization who conducts research for him or herself. Internal researchers can be grouped similarly to external researchers, with each internal-researcher group's unique requirements identified in a similar manner.

3.   **Proxy researcher (also referred to as knowledge broker)**

This individual is internal to an organization and performs research on behalf of another person who may be either internal or external. Proxy researchers are also placed into groups similar to those of the external researcher, with each proxy-researcher group's unique requirements identified in a similar manner.

6.2.4. Fast path = high risk

The basic tenet of KM is that people prefer fast information rather than best information: the so-called *fast path*. When performing KM analysis, therefore, it is necessary to identify that necessary knowledge is readily available, simple to find, and easy to understand and communicate. Immediacy is the key concern of a researcher; speed and quality are key concerns of the KM analysis process.

The drawback of the fast path the risk that information gained, and final decisions made, may not be researched and validated adequately. The fast path, therefore, is deemed to produce higher risk outcomes than the slow path. Despite the inherent risk of misinformation, the vast majority of decisions will be based on fast-path information.

Within the analysis, it is necessary to identify whether researchers (especially proxy researchers) have the necessary knowledge to fulfill immediate resolution. If not, it is necessary to identify what knowledge is needed and identify possible training requirements.

Beyond knowledge gained through personal experience, researchers will typically have only two courses of action when looking for information:

1. ask someone; or

2. use some type of technology such as computers, telephone and television, or through paper documentation.

On the fast path, organizations need to identify to whom (trusted advisors) or what (simple lookup systems) a researcher should turn for help. Organizations must also identify whether these resources can deliver the necessary information. When the necessary information is not available from these sources, organizations must identify how to update people and systems with the relevant supporting information.

An unwillingness to share knowledge is generally not a problem at this stage. If an employee demonstrates an unwillingness to share knowledge, he or she is not usually considered by a researcher to be part of his or her trusted advisors group. To identify trusted advisors, organizations must identify those individuals with whom the researcher has some form of existing relationship, or who are known to be willing to share what they know. Trusted advisors are most frequently found in the immediate physical vicinity of the researcher if he or she is categorized as being internal or proxy.

When searching for information, researchers are most likely to turn to simple-lookup technologies. The technologies are not necessarily electronic; they could also be books, manuals, microfiche, data sheets or poster boards. Identifying the capacity of people and systems to deliver simplicity, speed and quality is a key concern of the KM analysis process.

6.2.5. Fast- and slow-path transitions

Researchers in both fast and slow paths need to be aware of other participants. For example, performing a search on the simple-lookup database should provide not only required information, but also additional information on various trusted advisors with experience in the area or interest, as well methods of contacting these advisors. The simple-lookup database should also have hotlinks to subject-matter experts and additional advanced-research technologies.

Weights can be assigned to relationships established through simple-lookup technologies. Assigned weights influence the severity of risk associated with missing or corrupt links.

6.2.6. Slow path = low risk

The slow path is followed when the fast path fails to produce the required outcomes, and a researcher is willing to pursue his or her research and not draw conclusions based on what has been discovered or assumed to this stage. The slow path has the capability to provide broader and deeper access to both tacit experience and explicit information. With broader and deeper access comes complexity; with complexity comes latency.

Areas of potential latency:

- deciding which questions need to be asked;

- navigating and filtering experiences and information relevant to a specific business problem/solution set;

- identifying subject-matter experts (SMEs);

- lack of SME availability;

- willingness of SMEs to share information (time spent negotiating);

- potential need for language translation;

- time spent trying to find information repositories;

- time spent trying to understand what has been found;

- understanding how various pieces of information are inter-related;

- trying to prioritize importance of knowledge;

- size and scope of information repositories;

- how well existing information is codified;

- consistency in codification across multiple repositories; and

- whether information is located where researchers would naturally navigate to find it.

Although the slow path introduces latency for researchers, it also provides the highest level of experience and information. After slow-path research of an issue, a researcher will have gained more experience and information, leading to a more informed decision. For this reason, final decisions will also typically be lower risk than fast-path decisions.

6.2.7. People and technology

If researchers don't have enough confidence in their own knowledge to provide a solution, they have one of two recourses. The first is to turn to another person; the second is to turn to technology. KM analysis must follow both routes.

6.2.8. Trusted advisors

When turning to another person for help, researchers usually start by asking individuals they know, with whom they feel comfortable, and who typically shares their knowledge. Such an individual is considered a trusted advisor. In a corporate environment, a trusted advisor is usually someone with whom the researcher comes into regular contact, such as a departmental co-worker, project-team member, coffee-room cohort, or anyone with whom they physically interact with on a consistent basis. A trusted advisor can be located remotely, but is usually connected electronically via real-time technologies such as the Internet.

During KM analysis of trusted advisors, organizations must:

1. identify who is supporting a researcher real-time (list of trusted advisors);

2. identify which trusted advisors can play a role in the specific problem/solution set;

3. identify which knowledge trusted advisors have that supports the problem/solution set;

4. develop a knowledge map of what trusted advisors know against the problem/solution-set knowledge requirements to identify who knows what and who knows who. This is referred to as social-network analysis.

5. identify process and ownership requirements for keeping the map current and instantly available to a researcher;

6. identify attrition and succession issues with contingency planning;

7. identify other risks, issues and opportunities; and

8. identify if trusted advisors are aware of and transfer knowledge into simple-lookup technologies discussed in section 6.2.9: Simple-lookup systems.

6.2.9. Simple-lookup systems

The second course of action a researcher can take to resolve a problem/solution set is to turn to technology. Given that people prefer fast information to best information, simple-lookup systems must be fast. Once access and delivery speeds are satisfactory, issues of quality can be addressed.

KM analysis identifies:

1. which simple-lookup systems a researcher turns to first, such as paper, FAQ, knowledgebase, websites and search engines;

2. usability complaints and issues with existing simple-lookup systems;

3. how usability of simple-lookup systems could be improved;

4. alternative simple-lookup systems that could better serve a specific problem/solution set;

5. researchers' concerns over proposed new simple-lookup systems;

6. researchers' concerns about information quality;

7. information the simple-lookup systems are not supplying;

8. information that should be created, updated and abandoned;

9. if the simple-lookup systems also contain the trusted advisors map referenced in section 6.2.8: Trusted advisors; and

10. process and ownership requirements for maintaining speed of delivery and on-going sharing, sustainment, renewal and abandonment of information and technologies.

6.2.10. Subject-matter experts

Subject-matter experts (SMEs) follow the slow path. The KM analysis process requires that SMEs with integral knowledge of a particular problem/solution set be identified, and their knowledge mapped back to the knowledge requirements as discussed in the section 6.2.8: Trusted advisors. This information should then be used to update the simple-lookup technologies.

The KM analysis process should also address key concerns surrounding SMEs including:

1. location;

2. spoken and written language;

3. accessibility;

4. level of compensation;

5. rewards for sharing; and

6. capture and codification of knowledge transferred.

6.2.11. Advanced research systems

Advanced research systems come in many different forms. The list of systems is exhaustive and dynamic, and this document cannot hope to itemize them all. However, advanced-research tools available today include:

1. collaborative tools;

2. business-intelligence tools;

3. artificial-intelligence tools;

4. decision matrices;

5. metadata tools; and

6. social network tools.

Advanced research systems fall into the slow path because of their complexity and the volume of information available, both of which introduce latency into research.

During KM analysis, advanced research systems are used to identify:

1. available technologies;

2. usability complaints and issues with existing technologies;

3. how usability of technologies could be improved;

4. alternative advanced research systems that could possibly better serve the problem/solution set;

5. concerns about proposed new advanced research systems;

6. concerns about quality of information;

7. which information is not being supplied;

8. which information should be created, updated and abandoned;

9. process and ownership requirements to maintain content quality and on-going sharing, sustainment, renewal and abandonment of information and technologies

6.2.12. Communities of Practice (CoPs)

One of the most significant tools in a researcher's toolbox is the social network to which he or she has access. Communities of practice formalize this social network and extend it to accommodate issues of SME attrition, willingness to share and availability. Communities of practice focus on specific areas, such as nuclear medicine; therefore, multiple CoPs may be necessary to span an entire problem/solution set. The KM analysis framework identifies social networks and provides researchers with access to these networks.

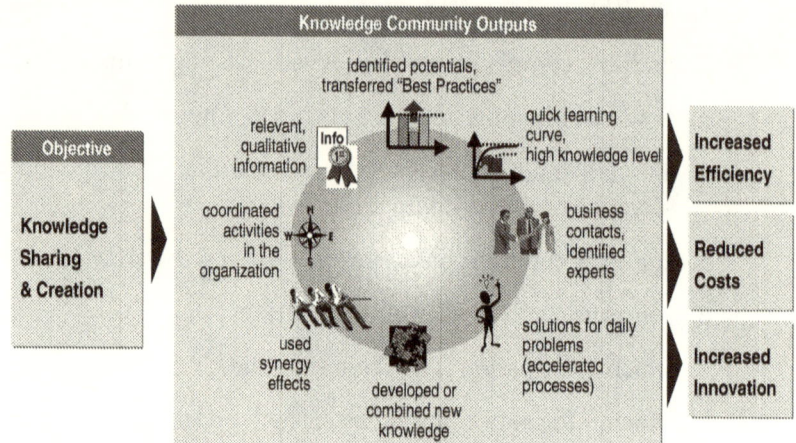

ILLUSTRATION 17: COMMUNITIES OF PRACTICE—MODIFIED SIEMENS CORP.

Some CoPs are organized horizontally; some operate vertically.

Horizontal communities aggregate people with similar functions across departments and, potentially, government. Sharing a specific problem or goal through a diverse community returns a better variety of experience and can reduce staffing requirements through shared resources. As an example, a new project requires three geologists, but the unit involved has only one. Shared resources enables the 'borrowing' of time from geologists in other departments depending on workload and knowledge, and eliminates the need to hire additional geologists. This type of knowledge sharing also helps to build redundancy across departments while improving cross-functional communications and awareness of what's happening in other organizational agencies and departments.

Vertical communities unite individuals with common goals, and ensure that members are aware of and engaged in all organization aspects necessary to achieving the goals. Decisions are made based on the combined inputs of all community members, which greatly mitigates risk. Virtual communities build an organic knowledgebase of lessons learned, best practices and experiences. The lessons learned can then be utilized repeatedly to replicate functionality on projects of a similar nature, significantly mitigating risk and making it easy to identify subject-matter experts. Once best practices are documented, they can be reviewed and fine-tuned using conventional scientific business-engineering techniques to create even better practices.

Illustration 18 shows a project-oriented community of practice.

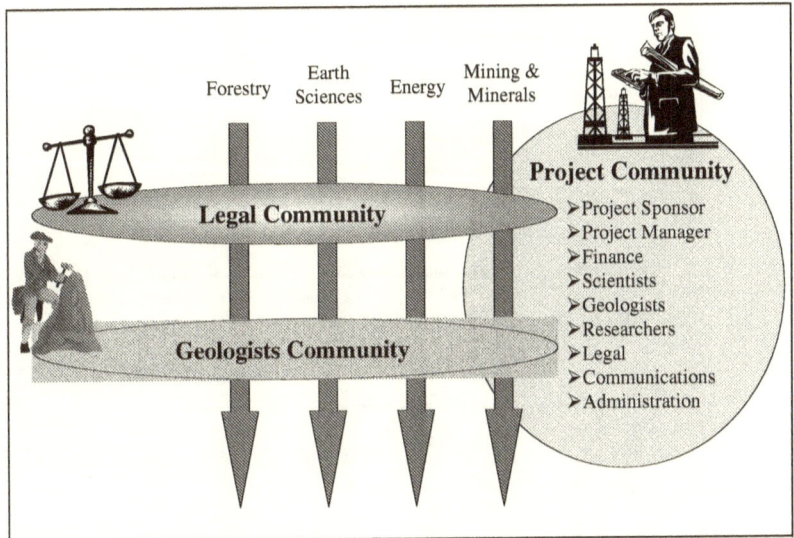

ILLUSTRATION 18: HORIZONTAL AND VERTICAL COMMUNITIES OF PRACTICE

6.2.13. Feedback systems

The KM analysis process identifies methods and processes to enable employees and systems to evolve. These methods and processes are called feedback systems or reentrant algorithms. In a perfect world this function would be automated; however, feedback systems will fail eventually and require upgrading so there will always be a measure of manual intervention required.

6.3. KM assessment and determination

The second aspect of the diagnostic methodology is KM assessment and determination. The output of assessment and determination is a KM recommendations report.

KM Solution Matrix

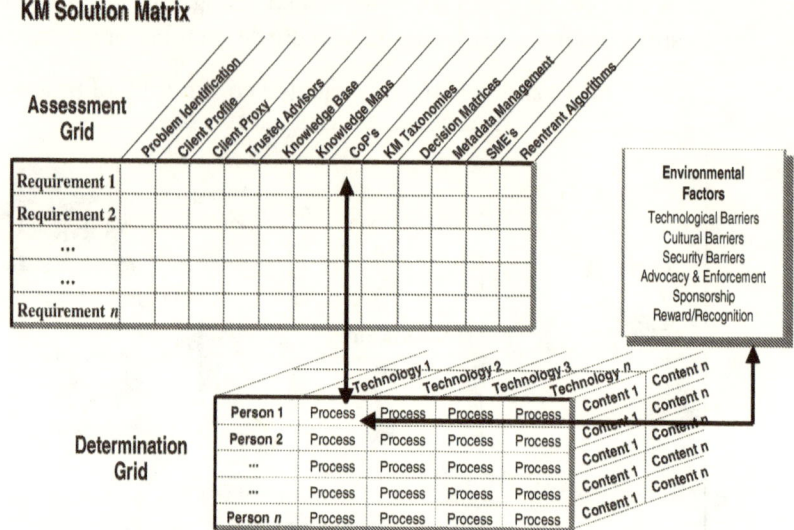

ILLUSTRATION 19: KM ASSESSMENT AND DETERMINATION GRIDS

6.3.1. Assessment grid

The assessment grid breaks down each of the knowledge requirements identified during the analysis process. The grid is a table that incorporates currently recognized methodologies for fulfilling various KM requirement types.

As an example, requirement one of the grid identifies that a certain subject-matter expert is soon to retire, that the SME's knowledge is crucial and unique, and that he or she is the only employee in the business unit to understand the knowledge fully. Such a situation constitutes a serious threat to the health of the affected business process.

Identification of the potential problem enables managers to identify SMEs, either inside or outside the organization, who may have similar knowledge, and be able to offset loss of the primary SME.

The assessment grid identifies potential KM solution methodologies to recognize and solve such individual problems. Each of the methodologies is analyzed further using the determination grid.

6.3.2. Determination grid

The determination grid divides proposed methodologies into individual solution components of people, processes, technologies and content. Each component is addressed independently and from an overall integration aspect.

Output from the determination grid may be several potential solution recommendations, each identified by impact, such as cost, time, scope and risk.

6.3.3. Environmental factors

Each of the potential solution recommendations must be weighed against organizational environmental factors including:

- technological barriers;
- cultural barriers;
- security barriers;
- advocacy and enforcement barriers;
- sponsorship barriers; and
- reward and recognition barriers.

7. VALUATION OF INTELLECTUAL ASSETS

The valuation of an intellectual asset will forever be subjective. However, when feeding management planning and assessing risk there is no doubt that valuation of intellectual assets is one of the most crucial yet difficult tasks in any knowledge-based organization.

The viability of many organizations is directly dependent on perceived value. However, intellectual (knowledge) assets are intangible and make valuation of any intellectual-asset-based organization complicated and interpolative. Many of today's organizations, including government agencies, are deemed to have, or provide, value often because of their intellectual assets.

Intellectual-asset-based organizations face a conundrum: they must find a way to value, measure and manage intangible assets, but little is available in the way of tools or training, even within internationally accepted systems such as GAAP (generally accepted accounting principles).

Without tools to value, measure and report on intellectual assets, governments' citizen populations and private-sector organizations' customers and shareholders will be unable to perceive the real value and potential of those organizations whose value is bound intrinsically to their inventory of intangible assets.

No standardized tools currently exist to deal with intangible-asset valuation, measurement and reporting. Tools such as GAAP deal with tangible assets only. GAAP even shows weaknesses when valuing, measuring and managing the intangible aspects of physical assets. For example, a piece of real estate (tangible asset) is purchased for $100k. Later, the real estate becomes attractive to buyers, but there is no way to recognize the increase in value (intangible gain) and indicate this gain on a balance sheet.

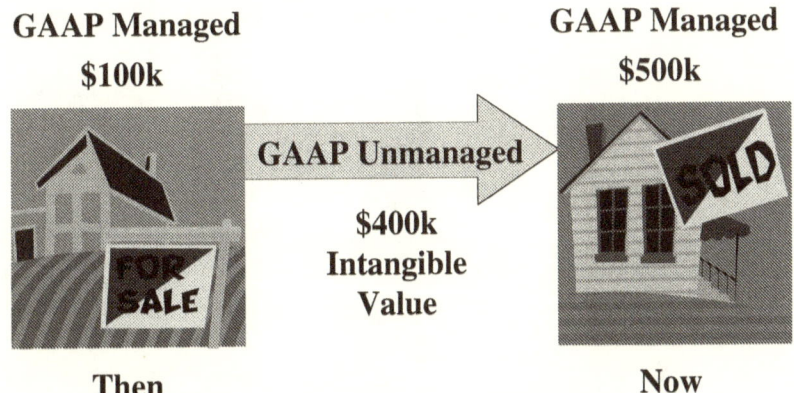

GAAP Managed   **GAAP Managed**

$100k   **$500k**

GAAP Unmanaged

$400k
Intangible
Value

Then   **Now**

ILLUSTRATION 20: WEAKNESSES IN GAAP

Even if identical properties to the real estate in question sell for $500k, GAAP recognizes the cost only, and any increase in value is recognized only when the property is sold. In this example, any perceived additional value over the original purchase cost is determined by assessing the value of recent property sales of similar types and nature within the same area. By combining this information with a variety of other less tangible factors a realistic value is predicted. At the moment of sale, the intangible gain becomes tangible and can be recognized on the balance sheet. The GAAP organization is attempting to address this problem, but has not even begun to address the problem of valuing intangible assets.

Organizations dependent on intellectual assets need a method to value and report on intangible assets today. Attempts are being made to develop measurement metrics for internal valuation, but none have yet been accepted by or adopted across multiple organizations. The reason for this lack of universal tools and techniques is simple: **valuation of something intangible is highly speculative.**

The following illustration presents a proposed methodology for analyzing the value of an intellectual asset:

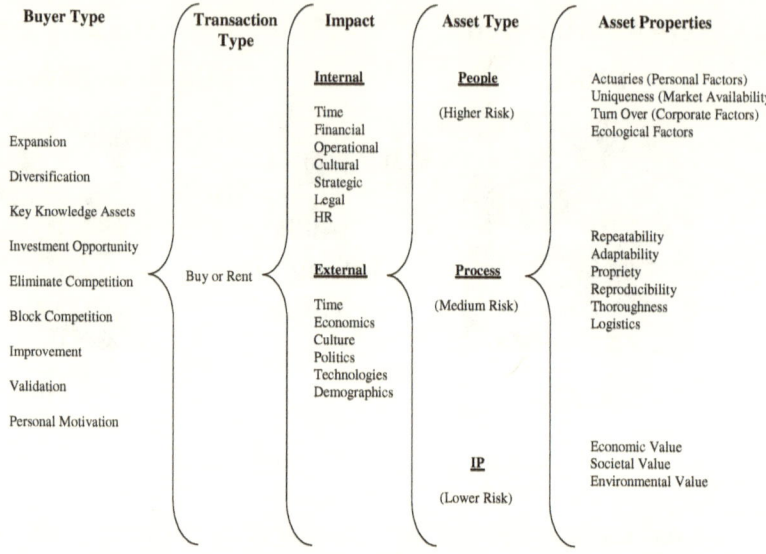

Buyer Type	Transaction Type	Impact	Asset Type	Asset Properties
		Internal	**People**	Actuaries (Personal Factors)
			(Higher Risk)	Uniqueness (Market Availability)
		Time		Turn Over (Corporate Factors)
Expansion		Financial		Ecological Factors
		Operational		
Diversification		Cultural		
		Strategic		
Key Knowledge Assets		Legal		
		HR		
Investment Opportunity				Repeatability
				Adaptability
Eliminate Competition	Buy or Rent	**External**	**Process**	Propriety
				Reproducibility
Block Competition		Time	(Medium Risk)	Thoroughness
		Economics		Logistics
Improvement		Culture		
		Politics		
Validation		Technologies		
		Demographics		
Personal Motivation				
				Economic Value
			IP	Societal Value
				Environmental Value
			(Lower Risk)	

ILLUSTRATION 21: ESTIMATING THE VALUE OF AN INTELLECTUAL ASSET

Before expanding each of these factors into a more detailed description it is prudent to note that this method of estimating is exactly that, a method. And a method is simply a means or manner of procedure; a regular and systematic way to accomplish a desired end.

This method of valuation attempts to provide analysts with a systematic way to dissect and evaluate the various constituent components that might affect the value of an intangible asset. The method can be expanded or contracted to suit a specific asset and the individual characteristics of an organization or audience. Each component of the analysis presents one or more impacts, and each level of impact is in turn affected by the ranking (or weight of impact) of the context of the perspective role. It is important that the analyst recognize—and factor into the valuation—that a valuation can be viewed from three possible perspective roles: buyer, seller and, potentially, broker. Each role will likely value the asset differently. After recognizing that the three roles generate three different perspectives of value, the job of valuation begins by breaking down the intellectual asset into various categories to analyze its constituent parts

7.1. Buyer Type

Before the details of an intellectual asset can be assessed, it is logical to determine the buyer type. If there is no potential buyer, the asset has no value. Each buyer type also has different motivations and these motivations are a major factor in determining how valuable any particular asset is. For example, an individual desperate for an intellectual asset will likely pay or sacrifice more to obtain it than someone who is only casually looking at the asset as a possible opportunity.

7.2. Transaction Type

Any asset, tangible or intangible, will usually demonstrate more value to an individual or organization looking to acquire it outright, rather than to an individual or organization looking to rent, borrow or simply leverage it.

7.3. Impact

The valuation of an intellectual asset is generally affected by its level of impact on various internal and external people, processes, technologies and content.

7.4. Asset Type

Intellectual assets can be broken down into three major categories: people, process and intellectual property. Each category has an effect on the valuation of an asset according to the level of associated risk.

7.5. People (highest risk)

When intellectual assets are related to people, the assets are typically associated with the highest level of risk because of the unpredictability of humans.

7.6. Process (medium risk)

When intellectual assets are related to process there is a medium level of risk associated, depending on the various factors surrounding the process. For example, any process that can be duplicated easily is of less value than a highly secret, complex process. However, if the process is designed to be duplicated, such as filling out a tax return, then the value of the process is related directly to the ease of duplication. Depending on the application of the processes, therefore, value and risk can mean very different things.

7.7. Intellectual Property (lowest risk)

Intellectual Property is usually defined as "anything defensible by law" and carries with it less associated risk than process or people. Assets such as patents, trademarks, copyrights and branding all fall into this category.

7.8. Asset Properties

Possibly the most complex part of analyzing any intellectual asset is interpreting associated properties. For example, with the "people" asset type, the methodology lists "Actuaries" as a property requiring analysis. Actuaries can then be broken down into many layers of complexity ranging from simple analysis, such as a person's age and gender, to complex analysis, such as the formulas used by insurance companies. In all asset types, a greater degree of certainty about the various asset properties directly lowers risk, increasing the accuracy of the valuation. Analysis itself does not necessarily increase the value of an asset; it simply helps to remove uncertainty about the value. An asset's properties are the most interpretive, and are also the primary point of controversy among the three primary roles of buyer, seller and broker.

By following the methodology, valuation analysts can assign their own priorities and weighted ranks to each factor. Used as a master check list, the valuation methodology leaves room for individualization, but provides a consistent approach to research that can be duplicated easily across multiple organizations and industries, and yet remain abstracted enough to apply to intellectual assets of any type or nature.

8. COMPLEX SYSTEMS

The basis of a complex system can probably be best described by relating it to something people may be familiar with. The following story of two vehicles passing in the night (which will be referred to as the "moment of incident") may help to clarify.

It's a dark stormy night and John is driving his car down a two-lane highway on route to his cottage for the weekend. The highway is fairly narrow and bordered with trees about 30 feet back from the edge of the road. Off in the distance John sees approaching headlights. He's listening to the radio and enjoying a snack he brought along for the trip. John had a long day at work and the drone of the rain on the windshield and the repetitive humming of the windshield wipers are making him feel a bit groggy. Still, the mood is relaxed and things appear fairly predictable to John.

8.1. Variables and Relationships

At this point in time John is living within a "simple system". He has no major decisions that need to be made, and the process of driving is pretty much routine. John only needs to make minor corrections to his steering as he zooms down the highway but is steadily moving towards a "moment of incident". The moment of incident is the point time where the analyst (in this case John) wants to predict probability of outcome, but that's a

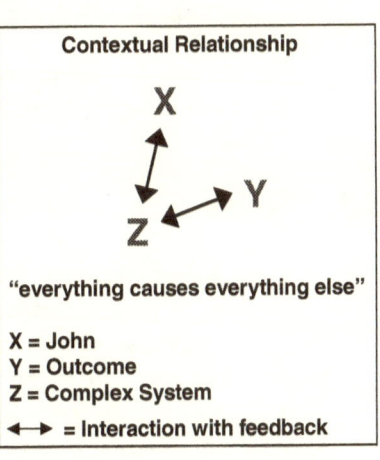

Contextual Relationship

X

Y

Z

"everything causes everything else"

X = John
Y = Outcome
Z = Complex System
←→ = Interaction with feedback

bit further down the road yet. At the moment, John only has to deal with a few general details (large-scale variables) such as road, rain, speed, oncoming vehicle and trees. He also needs to keep in mind a few rudimentary and loosely threaded relationships (car to road, car to oncoming vehicle, rain to road, light conditions to eyes, rain to car, speed to car). Some of these general details (large-scale variables) bear no or small relationships with other general details (trees to road, trees to car, speed to trees, etc.) At this point we can say that system stress level is low.

A short time later John can now see that the oncoming headlights belonging to some type of large truck. He knows this because he can see little orange lights all around the cab and trailer. The road is narrow so in the back of John's mind he starts contemplating the width of the truck, the width of his car, and the relationship between these widths and the width of the road. He also begins factoring in the potential impact of wind on his car that would be generated by a large truck passing at high speed and close range. John also considers the slippery road conditions brought on by the rain and the poor visibility brought on by the darkness and rain combined. He glances at the edge of the road to see if there is a paved shoulder just in case he needs to move over and give the truck a bit more room. John doesn't like the way the trucks headlights are set on high beam because the light sparkles like small sunbursts through the rain on his windshield. Because he's tired, John also begins to wonder whether or not the driver of the truck might also be tired and potentially falling asleep at the wheel so he sits up and starts paying closer attention. He flicks his headlights back and forth between high beam and low-beam several times to signal the truck driver to turn down the trucks headlights.

John is now becoming more "aware of the moment" and the system stress is increasing. With increased stress comes increased complexity.

8.2. Stress

What is stress? Stress is the agent or agents causing change. Like applying heat to water. Heat is the "stress" agent and water is the "system". The more stress is increased the hotter the water gets. Water is the "system" because that is the primary focus of what's being analyzed in order to predict potential outcomes. There may be multiple stress agents but there is only one system under analysis.

For instance, if this case study were focused on something other than two approaching vehicles, such as the impact of sunshine on the trees beside the highway, then the primary stress agent in that case would be "sunlight". Anything John does on the highway will have little to do with any "system" that we would be analyzing the impact of sunlight, unless John's car reflected sunlight onto the trees, then John's car would become a variable and then there would be some type of relationship between John's car and the system being analyzed. Since it's nighttime in this story, a system that focuses on the impact of sunlight on trees would be at low stress. Stress would increase at dawn in that case.

In John's case the primary stress agent is "time". As time passes, with each increment John is getting closer and closer to the truck, until eventually the level of stress reaches a critical point "the moment of incident" when the vehicles need to physically pass each other going opposite directions. As the clock ticks and John gets closer to the truck there is more and more details (variables) to take into consideration, so the "system" becomes more complex (more detailed). Eventually, if all goes well, John will pass the truck and the system stress will diminish accordingly and the system will once again get simpler (less detailed) the further John gets from the truck.

Therefore, we can expand on definition of "stress" as being the catalyst that stimulates the creation and destruction of variables (details). Large-scale variables are abstract, fuzzy and provide little detail while hiding the smaller, more focused details inside until such time that increasing levels of stress starts to expose them. As stress increases the large-scale variables start to disappear being replaced by a growing quantity of more and more granular variables (smaller and more focused details).

John is the analyst in this case. He is attempting to predict the outcome of the "moment of incident" when both vehicles will pass each other. Because time is the primary agent of change in this specific system, more details will appear than disappear as the vehicles approach each other, and determination of which details really matter or not becomes more complicated with each increment in time.

How is the level of importance determined for each variable? Answer = "Context"

8.3.   Context

The "context" is the set of facts or circumstances that surround the "current" situation. In order to understand the level of importance that any one particular variable has in relation to the current situation the analyst needs to assess what relationships each variable might have with any other variables. Therefore, it's the "context of the moment" that creates, destroys, weighs and reinforces new relationships between variables. As the system moves out of one context and into the next context, the quantity of variables and their associated relationships can change dramatically.

In this case, because we are looking at two vehicles moving towards each other, "Time" becomes the primary factor that influences the context. The more time that passes, the closer the vehicles get to each other. The closer the vehicles get to each other the greater increase in stress on the system caused by an increase in variables (level of available detail) and relationships between variables that need to be managed. The more detail available the more complicated it gets to determine what really matters and what doesn't "at this particular moment in time".

As the context continues to change, new variables and relationships are "dynamically" created, related and weighted. This means that, because the context is subject to change in complex systems, any approach to analyzing the system must also be dynamic to accommodate new variables and relationships as they appear or to anticipate the potential variables and relationships before they appear.

8.4. Unpredictability

Another factor that comes into play when analyzing a complex system is "unpredictability". Unpredictability exists in every complex system, and will increase in a non-linear fashion from nominal to overwhelming as complexity increases. In this case John is now beginning to contemplate whether the truck driver could be falling asleep at the wheel. John has no way of predicting what the truck driver will do or whether the truck driver is even awake, but at least he knows about the existence of this variable and can factor this variable and its various relationships into his mental analysis as being unpredictable. Just knowing of this variables existence and basic nature might be enough to trigger John to exercise additional caution. John might look to see if the truck is on the correct side of the road, or whether or not the truck is weaving back and forth over the line. Regardless of the knowledge

John brings to bear on this particular variable, the fact is that John cannot definitively determine or forecast the status or actions of the truck driver in this context.

8.5. The Unknown

The final and universal factor that exists in any complex system is "The Unknown". The unknown is a certainty. There will always be variables and relationships that the analyst will not know about that will play a part and interact with the context in a complex system. Just knowing that there are always unknown variables and relationships allows the analyst to forecast a margin of error in any projected outcome. The certainty of the unknown reinforces that systems of analysis of complex systems must be dynamic.

As John nears the oncoming truck a deer leaps out into the middle of the highway. John's mind kicks into overdrive as his brain attempts to deal with this new situation. He hadn't expected this to happen. Now John must decide whether to hit the brakes, hit the deer, or try to swerve out of the way. He sees the truck begin to swerve and John begins to panic. Adrenalin explodes into his veins and John's body (yet another complex system with its own variables, relationships, unpredictability and the unknown) predicts its own private outcome and responds accordingly to produce a preprogrammed output of its own. His foot slams the brake pedal and his hands wrench the steering wheel sending the car spinning off the edge of the highway.

The story ends here because the moment John left the highway he entered a different complex system. The oncoming truck has passed by John, so that complex system is diminishing into simplicity while John's current situation is increasing in complexity. In the new complex system John is just entering, velocity, weight and inertia will now take over as the stress agents and will control the context of the moment.

In the final chapter of John's saga, just prior to him spinning off the highway, an unknown variable became known and had the dynamic effect of massively reorganizing relationships between many variables. It even affected complex systems within the current complex system when John's body was required to fall back into "conditioned response" when his mind became overwhelmed with the task of managing the explosion of new variables, relationships, unpredictability and unknowns introduced by the sudden emergence of the deer.

What happened to John was just one of theoretically an infinite number of "what if" scenarios that might have played out.

8.6. Properties of a Complex System

So what can be stated about complex systems?

1. The incident is the focus of the observation

2. The further away from the incident the simpler the system

3. The moment of incident is the window of time to be analyzed from which we want to predict outcomes

4. Stress is the change agent applied to a complex system

5. Change is directly bound to time

6. A change in stress is accompanied by a directly related non-linear change in complexity

7. Complexity is proportional to the quantity of variables, relationships, unpredictability, and the Unknown available within the system

8. The presence and configuration of variables, relationships, unpredictability and the Unknown determines the context

9. The presence, configuration, state and weights of the variables, relationships, unpredictability and the Unknown, at any point in time, is the "context of the moment"

10. It's the interaction of all components within the context of the moment that determines the potential outcomes at that moment

11. Unpredictability and The Unknown are certain

12. There are theoretically an infinite number of potential outcomes

13. The more variables and relationships that can be analyzed, and the closer we can bring unpredictability and the Unknown to zero, the more accurate the prediction of the outcomes

14. Variables, relationships, unpredictability and the Unknown can be weighted as factors in analysis

15. Variables, relationships, unpredictability and the Unknown can be influenced

16. Complex systems are dynamic

17. Complex systems require dynamic analysis to predict potential outcomes

18. Influencing Variables, relationships, unpredictability and the Unknown within a complex system can affect the outcomes

8.7. Dynamic Management of Knowledge within a Complex System

Large volumes of work have been published on complex systems and many models have been designed to assist in rationalizing, predicting and controlling outcomes. These models usually fall into two major categories of approach and have factors that affect the nature of their design and implementation:

8.7.1. Conceptual Models

Conceptual models are founded on intuitive reasoning based on experience where the models extract the most relevant variables, relationships, unpredictability factors and unknowns and produce models based on a level of abstraction from the potentially huge volumes of data that may be available. These models are very flexible to adapt to unforeseen changes and generalize easily to qualitatively new situations.

8.7.2. Analytical Models

Analytical Models attempt to include as many variables, relationships, unpredictability factors and unknowns as can be perceived or postulated and apply analytical calculations to eliminate redundant data in an attempt to develop the most detailed model possible. These models are typically not very flexible and don't accommodate highly dynamic systems very well. Having said that, if the system if fairly static these models provide the highest level of certainty. The obvious weakness using this type of model in a highly dynamic system stems from the high likelihood that conclusions might be reached based on old data.

With these two approaches in mind, then within highly dynamic complex systems it is recommended to use simple, intuitive, low-dimensional models with local and short-term predictability that allow the analysts to conceptualize a complex system without significant formalization. In less dynamic complex systems it would likely serve better to use extremely detailed, high-dimensional models with either local or global and either short or long-term predictability that demands the input of the largest number of parameters with their associated data that is as close to real-time as possible.

Both models can be augmented through the use of computational models that can provide simulation testing and "what if" scenarios.

The balance of this section will discuss one method of designing a Conceptual Model. Analytical models are beyond the scope of this document.

8.8. Developing and Implementing a Conceptual Model

The following model is designed as a method of approach for organizational decision-making. This model is only one example of a conceptual model and is designed to assist decision-makers by using a loosely formal matrix for decision-making in dynamic environments. The model adopts a "question-based" approach that can allow experts (researchers) in each area to respond and assimilate their associated confidence into a computational model. This approach is designed to leverage the collective expertise of the assigned research team, capture and codify context sensitive knowledge and potentially leverage historical knowledge that may exist from previous decisions. This combined knowledge can be brought to bear on a complex system to analyze both the problem and solution potentials in a systematic fashion.

In order to build a conceptual model for predicting or influencing potential outcomes of a highly dynamic complex system the modeler needs knowledge gained from:

1. human experience

2. identification of the incident (focus of the observation)

3. identification of the moment of incident (the window of time the analyst is interested in with regards to the incident)

4. identification of or postulation of the presence, configuration, state and weights of pre, mid and post variables and relationships

5. estimation of the impact of pre, mid and post unpredictability in variables and relationships

6. estimation of the potential impact from pre, mid and post unknowns

This model could be broken into two matrices:

1. Problem Analysis

2. Solution Analysis ("what if" scenarios)

Both matrices should provide feedback in terms of probability, which is measured as the level of confidence that the researchers have in the interpretation of the data made available to them. The conceptual model is a low-dimensional method of approach based on abstracted and perceived data and dependent on the researchers experience. Confidence is a significant method of associating weight to any particular matrix, node, analysis point, or relationship.

8.8.1. Problem Analysis

The problem analysis matrix targets the need to understand the fundamental nature of what problem needs to be solved. Too often decision-makers jump forward to debating various solutions without ever fully understanding the problem. There is nothing worse than spending time and resources finding the right answer to the wrong problem. The problem analysis matrix is attempting to understand the symptoms, deliver a diagnosis and postulate a prognosis using a consistent, yet loosely formal approach across all researchers.

The problem analysis matrix could be subdivided into six hi-order nodes:

1. What

2. Why

3. Who

4. When

5. Where

6. The Unknown

Each of the six hi-order nodes could then be broken into analysis points:

1. **What**

    a. What are the symptoms of the problem?

    b. What do we need to know to provide a reasonable diagnosis?

    c. What should we expect as outcomes on successful or failed resolution of this problem?

    d. What additional problems will this problem generate?

    e. What are the metrics that define success or failure?

    f. What dependencies impact this problem?

2. **Why**

    a. Why did this problem appear?

    b. Why are we in this predicament?

    c. Why do we consider this a problem?

    d. Why were we unable to predict this problem?

    e. Why do we need to take action on this problem?

    f. Why do we think this problem can be solved?

3. **Who**

    a. Who is creating or involved with generating the symptoms of this problem?

    b. Who needs to be engaged to analyze this problem?

    c. Who is positively and negatively impacted by the problem?

    d. Who influences the problem?

e. Who knows about the problem?

f. Who owns this problem and defines the metrics?

4. **When**

a. When will this problem manifest itself?

b. When has this problem happened before and what was done to resolve it then?

c. When does this problem need to be solved?

d. When does timing play a critical role throughout this problem?

e. When will this problem place a demand on our resources?

f. When do dependencies affect the problem?

5. **Where**

a. Where did or will this problem start?

b. Where did or will this problem spread to?

c. Where is the anticipated or realized point of maximum impact?

d. Where do we find research materials to support this problem analysis?

e. Where can we test and measure for data input to problem analysis?

f. Where do we go from here (next steps)?

6. **The Unknown**

a. What don't we know?

b. Why don't we know?

c. How do we find out?

d. Who is looking into it?

e. Where are they looking?

f. When will we know?

8.8.2. Solution Analysis

The solution analysis matrix targets the need to explore potential solutions to the problem and probe potential probability of outcomes. Most decision-makers today are familiar with problem resolution practices but there is little in the way of consistency of approach. The solution analysis matrix provides for an informal but structured methodology to approach problem resolution analysis.

The solution analysis matrix could also be subdivided into six hi-order nodes:

1. What

2. How

3. When

4. Who

5. Where

6. The Unknown

Each of the six hi-order nodes could then be broken into analysis points:

1. **What**

   a. What is the proposed solution?

   b. What makes this solution better than any alternative?

   c. What do we need to do to implement the solution?

   d. What are the anticipated positive and negative outcomes?

   e. What are the metrics that define success or failure?

   f. What dependencies impact this solution?

2. **How**

   a. How much will this solution cost?

   b. How much money will this solution save or make us?

   c. How much time will this solution take to implement?

   d. How does this solution support the organizations mission and objectives?

   e. How does this solution support the organizations strategy?

   f. How does this solution align with our core competencies?

3. **When**

   a. When will funding be required?

   b. When can we expect a return on investment?

   c. When can implementation begin?

   d. When can implementation be completed?

   e. When can we begin to see the problem start vanishing?

   f. When will the problem be solved completely?

4. **Who**

   a. Who is funding the solution?

   b. Who will own this solution?

   c. Who is positively and negatively impacted by this solution?

   d. Who needs to be engaged to analyze this solution?

   e. Who needs to be engaged to implement this solution?

   f. Who needs to be engaged to sustain this solution?

5. **Where**

   a. Where is the funding coming from?

   b. Where is the funding being allocated?

   c. Where is the anticipated point of maximum impact?

   d. Where do we test and measure for success or failure?

   e. Where do we find research materials to support this solution?

   f. Where do we go from here (next steps)?

6. The Unknown

   a. What don't we know?

   b. Why don't we know?

   c. How do we find out?

   d. Who is looking into it?

   e. Where are they looking?

   f. When will we know?

8.8.3. Commonalities within in the Matrices

8.8.3.1. Confidence as a Measure of Probability

Each analysis point (detailed variable) within a node (larger-scale variable) is bound to the other analysis points via various types of relationships and each relationship carries with it its own weight in the form of confidence level. The aggregated total weight of all analysis points and relationships is then "bubbled up" from the various analysis points to the node. Each node in turn is bound to the other nodes through a variety of different types and weighted relationships. All nodes also "bubble up" their aggregated weights to the overall top level matrix (the complex system) where the totals become representative of the overall probability determined by the confidence in the understanding of the problem or proposed solution.

8.8.3.2. Relationships

In this specific example the model designers can predefine the relationships because there is a reasonable level of predictability of the interrelationships within the matrix, and between the nodes and the analysis points. Each relationship can be pre-assigned a default weight.

8.8.3.3. Risks, Issues and Opportunities

Although, in this model, relationships can be reasonably pre-established, there will always be a measure of unpredictability and the unknown with regards to variables and relationships. The overall confidence of any particular matrix, node, analysis point or relationship can be subjected to adjustment by the recognition of risks, issues or opportunities. Therefore the model must accommodate and ability to affect analysis results at any level of the matrix, or across the matrix as a whole, to modify probability scores accordingly and identify the nature of the risk, issue or opportunity.

8.8.3.4.   Capturing Context

With every piece of data analyzed within the model there should be a method of storing detailed levels of context. Within a highly dynamic complex system, what is relevant is only relevant now. But having said that, it's not the output of the analysis that provides organizational value alone. The model should recognize that both human experience and organizational knowledge are being brought to bear on the problem/solution and should do its utmost to capture and codify how this experience and knowledge was incorporated and leveraged, who provided the knowledge, the details of trials and tribulations that were discussed and resolved, how adversity was overcome, what could have been done better, and what should and shouldn't happen next time. This type of knowledge is ripe for codification into technological systems that manage this process, but it needs to be stored in the context that it was viewed or created.

At some point in time, should a similar problem present itself in a different context, or should a completely different problem be approached, context sensitive historical knowledge could then be integrated, analyzed and possibly leveraged. Therefore the model should be designed to accommodate, as part of its fundamental structure, the inclusion of context sensitive historical organizational knowledge.

With the implementation of various technologies and processes organizations could utilize artificial intelligence, statistical analysis and/or data warehousing analyses techniques to probe this "context aware" historical knowledgebase to identify possible patterns that may provide valuable clues to help on new problems or potentially expose areas of strength, weakness or trends the organization was not aware of. One very powerful use of the output of this type of cross-context analysis would be to use the feedback to adjust the weights of variables and relationships based on what level of impact they had within a specific context and how their existence affected probability scores. Variables and Relationships could then be reinforced, removed or realigned based on recognized patterns.

There is no limit to how people and technology may utilize context sensitive knowledge, but without archiving what we learn as we go, especially in the context that it was learned, it would be of no benefit to the organization if the knowledge were lost.

8.9.   Influencing Outcomes

Modeling complex systems is similar to throwing pebbles into a pond. Throw in only a couple or pebbles and their resultant waves, and the interference patterns created when the different waves collide, as well as the outcomes, are fairly predictable. But making complex decisions isn't like that; it's messy. Throw in a handful of pebbles and it would take some decent Newtonian physics to predict the interference patterns and outcomes.

But we can influence the outcomes if we target specific waves and amplify them by throwing a bigger rock in exactly where we want and then watch the big wave render many little waves practically inconsequential. In the case of John in our earlier example, driving his car on a rainy night, if we could have influenced the deer to pause for a minute or two before jumping onto the highway John would have probably experienced a completely different outcome.

This conceptual model should allow decision-makers to computationally test "what if" scenarios fairly quickly and easily. It should also help identify and/or exploit potential strengths and weaknesses in variables and relationships. With this ability, decision-makers could influence one or more variables or relationships and potentially develop and entirely new approach to resolving a problem.

9. CONCLUSION

Intellectual (knowledge) assets are the primary capital of the Government of Canada, and need to be managed like any other corporate asset. Treasury Board has laid out the necessary changes that are needed to bring Government asset management in line with modern management practices; accordingly these aspects of modern comptrollership are now embedded in deputy ministers' performance criteria. The COSO Learning and Development Committee's report in July of 2002 stated, "A results-based organization requires a new management model. Knowledge management and people are two essential cornerstones of a new public sector management model."

However, a number of questions must be asked before time and resources are invested in knowledge management: Why implement knowledge management? Where will KM take organizations? How will KM help achieve personal and organizational goals?

9.1. Why manage knowledge?

Knowledge is embedded in all government services and products, as well as being a major ingredient in strategy and policy formulation, and program delivery. Knowledge management (KM) can help address the internal and external pressures that the Canadian government is facing with respect to the management of its intellectual assets. KM is practical, tangible and measurable, and can help organizations to reach beyond current boundaries to inspire innovation, performance and corporate growth.

KM is concerned with:

- management planning and risk management;

- people and the way they make decisions;

- knowledge sharing across many domains;

- people and the way they learn, remember and teach what government knows;

- the citizens of Canada being served and empowered with knowledge that helps them make life, business and social decisions; and

- incremental change and business transformation by leveraging available knowledge and information in more effective ways.

9.2.   Where can Knowledge Management take organizations?

Knowledge Management can help create learning-, remembering- and mentoring-based organizations to effectively pursue challenges in today's complex and rapidly changing global environment.

Knowledge Management provides the framework of people, processes and technology necessary to capture, transfer and enhance an organization's intellectual assets.

9.3.   What can Knowledge Management help to deliver?

Effective knowledge management enables:

- reduced risk and enhanced management planning;

- better decision making and higher service levels;

- enhanced sharing and re-use of knowledge across business lines;

- identification of knowledge resources and corporate knowledge domains; and

- the capture, transfer and retention of corporate knowledge.

0-595-30699-3